the Inviting WORD

**A Worship-centered, Lectionary-based
Curriculum for Congregations**

Learner's Guide for Youth

Year 3

United Church Press

Cleveland, Ohio

Thomas E. Dipko	Executive Vice President, United Church Board for Homeland Ministries
Audrey Miller	General Secretary, Division of Education and Publication
Lynne M. Deming	Publisher
Sidney D. Fowler	Editor for Curriculum Resources
Kathleen C. Ackley	Associate Editor for Curriculum Resources
Monitta Lowe	Editorial Assistant
Marjorie Pon	Managing Editor
Kelley Baker	Editorial Assistant
Paul Tuttle	Marketing Director
Linda Peavy	Associate Marketing Director
Madrid Tramble	Production Manager
Martha A. Clark	Art Director
Angela M. Fasciana	Sales and Distribution Manager
Marie Tyson	Order Fulfillment/Inventory Control Manager

Writers

Deborah Gline Allen, who wrote the lessons for Proper 17 through Proper 29, is the consultant for youth ministry for the New Hampshire Conference of the United Church of Christ.

Paul Forrey is a United Church of Christ pastor who is particularly devoted to Christian education and youth ministry. Lillian Valentin is also an ordained United Church of Christ pastor and has served in a variety of ecumenical settings. Lillian and Paul wrote the lessons for Advent 1 through Transfiguration Sunday.

Jana Norman-Richardson, the writer of the lessons for Lent 1 through Easter 7 and Proper 17 (cycle B), is a minister at the First Congregational Church in Winter Park, Florida, and a founding leader of the United Church of Christ Florida Conference Statewide Youth Committee.

Mariellen Sawada, an avid youth worker and advocate, is pastor of the Aldersgate United Methodist Church, a Japanese American congregation in Palo Alto, California. She wrote the lessons for Pentecost Sunday through Proper 16.

Editor

Nan Duerling, Ph.D., editor of older youth resources, is an active lay member of Linthicum Heights United Methodist Church in Maryland and a former English teacher who has been writing and editing church curriculum resources for youth and adults since 1984.

United Church Press, Cleveland, Ohio 44115
© 1996 by United Church Press

The Inviting Word has been designed to be used with the New Revised Standard Version of the Bible. All scripture quotations, unless otherwise noted, are from the New Revised Standard Version of the Bible, © 1989 by the Division of Christian Education of the National Council of Churches of Christ in the U.S.A. Adaptations have been made for clarity and inclusiveness. Used by permission.

Design

Kapp & Associates, Cleveland, Ohio

Cover art

Glen Strock, *Parable of the Talents*, detail, Dixon, New Mexico. Used by permission of the artist.

The Inviting Word helps you to recognize the gifts and talents God has entrusted to you. By faithfully using these gifts, you invite all of creation to experience God's love, peace, and justice.

Glen Strock, *Parable of the Talents*, Dixon, New Mexico.
Used by permission of the artist.

Welcome and Information Sheet

As you and your friends explore the Bible in the year ahead, you will discover that God has given gifts and empowered people just like you to do God's work in the world. The stories of the Bible record over and over again that God called and lives were changed when ordinary people said "yes" to God.

You are invited to come to each lesson with curiosity, creativity, questions, and a desire to seek the One who is always ready to work in and through you. As you study the Word and engage in experiences with art, music, and literature you may sense God's call on your own life. Dare to respond by making new promises and greater commitments to God. You too are one of God's people and you too can use your God-given gifts to change the world.

**To help your leaders nurture the group,
please complete the form below and return it to them.**

Name ....

Address ....

Telephone number ....

Birth date ....

Year in school ....

Parent(s) or guardian(s) ....

Address ....

Telephone number ....

Have you been baptized? If so, when and where? ....

....

If you were baptized as an infant, have you been confirmed? If so, when

and where? ....

What do you like most about worship? ....

....

....

What are your special interests or hobbies? ....

....

....

What talents would you be willing to share with this group? ....

....

....

What are your hopes for this group? ....

....

....

What do you hope to gain from an exploration of the Bible? ....

....

....

Contents

Lent (Cycle B)

Easter (Cycle B)

Pentecost (Cycle B)

Moses, Moses!

Moses looked, and the bush was blazing, yet it was not consumed. Then Moses said, "I must turn aside and look at this great sight, and see why the bush is not burned up." When God saw that Moses had turned aside to see, God called to him out of the bush, "Moses, Moses!"

Exodus 3:2b–4a

God's call

Going with the Word Litany

One: May the God of your ancestors,

All: the God of Abraham and Sarah,

the God of Isaac and Rebekah,

the God of Jacob, Leah, and Rachel,

One: be with you as you respond to God's call this week.

All: Amen.

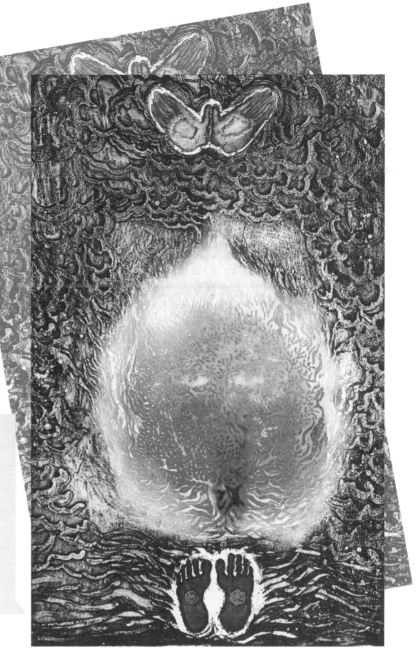

Paul Koli, *The Burning Bush*, as reproduced in *The Bible Through Asian Eyes*, ed. Masao Takenaka and Ron O'Grady (Auckland, New Zealand: Pace Publishing in association with the Asian Christian Art Association, 1991), 41. Used by permission of the Asian Christian Art Association.

If God were to **call you** *to do something today,* **what would it be?**

7

The Burning Bush Questionnaire

Answer the following questions by circling or writing in the best answer **for you**. The purpose of these questions is to help you think about the story of Moses' call and your own call while having a little fun at the same time.

1. If God were to call you to do something, what do you think you would be asked to do or to be?

a. A famous rock singer who gives all his or her money to those in need.

b. A world traveler who matches children who have no one to care for them with new families.

c. A well-known actor who stars in a Christian television show.

d. Your own answer:

_____

2. Why do you think God will call or has called you?

a. People always tell me how special I am.

b. I know I'm the greatest.

c. I believe that God calls everyone.

d. Your own answer:

_____

3. How do you see yourself as being like Moses?

a. I have a burning bush in my backyard.

b. I am curious about the unknown.

c. I don't think I can handle a big job God may have for me to do.

d. Your own answer:

_____

4. What concerns do you have about what others might think?

a. I'm afraid that my friends would make fun of me if I told them that God told me to do something.

b. I don't care what everyone else thinks; God is too important to me to let others run my life.

c. I'll do whatever God wants me to do, as long as my friends don't find out.

d. Your own answer:

_____

5. What would you say to God if God called you?

a. Who am I that you think I have what it takes to do a job for you?

b. I've got someone on the other line right now; could I get back to you?

c. I'm not sure I can do this job myself, but if you promise to be with me, sure, I'll do it.

d. Your own answer:

_____

6. What questions would you have for God about this call?

a. Why me?

b. Do I get to perform any miracles?

c. Do you promise to fix any mistakes I might make?

d. Your own answer:

_____

7. God promised to be with Moses while he freed the Israelites from slavery in Egypt. Since God promises to be with you as with Moses, what kind of thing can you imagine yourself doing with God's help?

a. I can help people in need and feel real good about myself and what I'm doing.

b. I will be liked by a lot of people because they'll see how wonderful I am!

c. I will be able to do things I'm usually afraid of doing.

d. Your own answer:

_____

8. Moses' main concern about carrying out God's call was fear—especially fear of how the people would react to him and fear of Pharaoh. God's promise to be with Moses helped to calm all his fears. What fears would you or do you have that God can calm?

a. I am afraid of being hurt by violent and angry people.

b. I am afraid that no one will like me.

c. I am afraid that there may not be a future for me.

d. Your own answer:

_____

9. What do you think God is calling you to do in the week ahead? Are you willing to accept this challenge?

Your answer:

_____

Festival of Freedom

This day shall be a day of remembrance for you. You shall celebrate it as a festival to God; throughout your generations you shall observe it as a perpetual ordinance.

Exodus 12:14

Adir Hu
God of Might

1 A - dir hu, a - dir hu, yiv-
1 God of might, God of right,
2 We en - slaved thus were saved

neh vei - to b' - ka - rov, bim - hei - ra
we would bow be - fore you, sing your praise
through God's might ap - pear - ing, so we pray

bim - hei - ra b' - ya - mei - nu, b' - ka - rov Eil b' - nei,
in these days, cel - e - brate your glo - ry, as we hear
for the day when we shall be hear - ing free - dom's call

eil b' - nei, b'nei veit - cha b' - ka - rov.
year by year, free - dom's won - drous sto - ry.
reach - ing all, the peo - ple's God re - ver - ing.

From Howard I. Bogot and Robert J. Orkand, *A Children's Haggadah* (New York: Central Conference of American Rabbis, 1994), 70. Used by permission.

WHY IS THIS NIGHT DIFFERENT FROM ALL OTHER NIGHTS?

✳ Haggadah Litany

This is an adaptation of the Passover Haggadah (which means "to tell"). This "telling" includes scripture, prayers, and explanations of the foods included in the annual Passover meal. This page only includes the explanation of the foods. The Passover celebration itself is much longer.

Light the candle on the table.

All: Thank you, God, for the festival light, and for bringing us together to celebrate the Passover.

Pour the grape juice into cups, one for each person, and pass them out to each person. When all are served, everyone may take a drink.

All: Thank you, God, for the grapes that grow to make this drink for our celebration.

Learners: Why is this night different from all other nights of the year? On all other nights we eat all kinds of bread and crackers. Why do we eat only matzo on the Passover? On all other nights we eat many kinds of vegetables and herbs. Why do we eat bitter herbs at our Passover? On all other nights we don't usually dip one food into another. At our Passover meal we dip the parsley in salt water and the bitter herbs in Charoset (HAR'O SET). Why do we dip foods twice tonight? On all other nights we eat sitting up straight. Why do we lean on a pillow tonight?

Leader: You have asked many questions. Let us search for the answers as we read and tell the story of the Passover as found in Genesis 37–50 and Exodus 1–11, 12:1–14.

If you are not present as the leader tells this story from the leader's guide, read Exodus 12:1–14 from your own Bible.

Leader: Now that we have told the story of the Passover, let us see if we can answer the questions you have asked.

Learners: Why do we eat only matzo on the Passover?

Leader: Matzo reminds us that when the Jewish people left Egypt, they had no time to bake bread for their journey. They put raw dough on their backs, and the sun baked it into hard crackers called matzo.

Learners: Why do we eat bitter herbs at our Passover?

Leader: The bitter herbs remind us of the bitter and cruel way Pharaoh treated the Jewish people when they were slaves in Egypt.

Learners: Why do we dip foods twice on the Passover?

Leader: We dip bitter herbs into the charoset to remind us how hard the Jewish slaves worked in Egypt. The chopped apples and nuts look like mortar, which were used to make bricks for building Pharaoh's cities and palaces. We dip parsley into salt water. The parsley reminds us that spring is here and new life will grow. The salt water reminds us of the tears of the Jewish slaves.

Learners: Why do we lean on a pillow at the Passover?

Leader: We recline as free people in order to be comfortable and to remind us that once we were slaves, but now we are free.

Pass around the matzo and invite each person to take a piece to eat. When all have eaten, say together:

All: Thank you, God, for the blessing of bread, and for the special matzo that reminds us of the Jewish people's hurried flight from Egypt.

Adapted from Judyth Saypol and Madeleine Wikler, *My Very Own Haggadah* (Rockville, Md.: Kar Ben Copies, Inc., 1974). Used by permission.

Through the *Sea*

Then Moses stretched out his hand over the sea. God drove the sea back by a strong east wind all night, and turned the sea into dry land, the waters were divided. The Israelites went into the sea on dry ground, the waters forming a wall for them on their right and on their left.

Exodus 14:21–22

Shalom of Safed, *The Exodus with the Pillar of Fire*, 1967, as reproduced in *Images from the Bible: The Words of Elie Wiesel, the Paintings of Shalom of Safed* (New York: The Overlook Press, 1980), 107. Paintings © 1980 by Shalom of Safed. Used by permission.

Suppose you were in this picture with the Israelites. How would you feel seeing the water in front of you and knowing the Egyptian army was behind you?

What "walls of water" confront you in your own life?

How would you feel when you saw that obstacles were removed in your own life, just as God parted the water for the Israelites?

*You are set **free** from your old ways, **washed** and refreshed by the **waters** of the ages.*

11

Crashing Waters at Creation

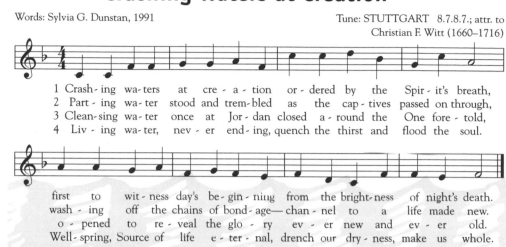

Words: Sylvia G. Dunstan, 1991

Tune: STUTTGART 8.7.8.7.; attr. to
Christian F. Witt (1660–1716)

1 Crash - ing wa - ters at cre - a - tion or - dered by the Spir - it's breath,
2 Part - ing wa - ter stood and trem - bled as the cap - tives passed on through,
3 Clean - sing wa - ter once at Jor - dan closed a - round the One fore - told,
4 Liv - ing wa - ter, nev - er end - ing, quench the thirst and flood the soul.

first to wit - ness day's be - gin - ning from the bright - ness of night's death.
wash - ing off the chains of bond - age— chan - nel to a life made new.
o - pened to re - veal the glo - ry ev - er new and ev - er old.
Well - spring, Source of life e - ter - nal, drench our dry - ness, make us whole.

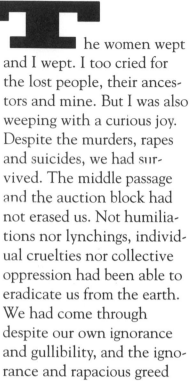

The women wept and I wept. I too cried for the lost people, their ancestors and mine. But I was also weeping with a curious joy. Despite the murders, rapes and suicides, we had survived. The middle passage and the auction block had not erased us. Not humiliations nor lynchings, individual cruelties nor collective oppression had been able to eradicate us from the earth. We had come through despite our own ignorance and gullibility, and the ignorance and rapacious greed of our assailants.

There was much to cry for, much to mourn, but in my heart I felt exalted knowing there was much to celebrate. Although separated from our languages, our families and customs, we had dared to continue to live. We had crossed the unknowable oceans in chains and had written its mystery into "Deep River, my home is over Jordan." Through the centuries of despair and dislocation, we had been creative, because we faced down death by daring to hope.

Maya Angelou, *All God's Children Need Traveling Shoes*
(New York: Random House, 1986), 207.

What does freedom mean to you?

Rain Down Bread

The whole congregation of the Israelites complained against Moses and Aaron in the wilderness. Then God said to Moses, "I am going to rain bread from heaven for you, and each day the people shall go out and gather enough for that day. In that way I will test them, whether they will follow my instruction or not."

Exodus 16:2, 4

In my dreams, I walk among the ruins
of the old part of town
looking for a bit of stale bread.

My mother and I inhale the fumes of gunpowder.
I imagine it to be the smell of pies, cakes, and kebab.

A shot rings out from a nearby hill. We hurry.
Though it's only nine o'clock, we might by hurrying
toward a grenade marked "ours."

An explosion rings out in the street of dignity.
Many people are wounded—
sisters, brothers, mothers, fathers.

I reach out to touch a trembling, injured hand.
I touch death itself.

Terrified, I realize this is not a dream.
It is just another day in Sarajevo.

Edina, 12, from Sarajevo, in *I Dream of Peace: Images of War by Children of Former Yugoslavia* (New York: HarperCollins, 1994), 47.
© 1994 UNICEF. Used by permission of HarperCollins Publishers, Inc.

How is God calling you to support those who are hungry?
What will you do?

Käthe Kollwitz, *Germany's Children Are Hungry! (Deutschlands Kinder Hungern!)*,
1924 lithograph, Rosenwald Collection, National Gallery of Art, Washington, D.C.
Used by permission.

13

The Manna shall fall by night.

As the Grains of Wheat

Words and music: Marty Haugen, 1991

As the grains of wheat once scat-tered on the hill were gath-ered in-to one to be-come our bread; so may all your peo-ple from all the ends of earth be gath-ered in-to one in you. you.

1 As this cup of bless-ing is
2 Let this be a fore-taste of

shared with-in our midst, may we share the pres-ence of your love.
all that is to come when all cre - a - tion shares this feast with you.

Tell the Glorious Deeds

We will not hide them
from their children;
we will tell to the coming
generations the glorious
deeds of God, and God's might,
and the wonders that
God has done.

Psalm 78:4

Our faith draws us together this day.
Let us trust enough to open our ears and our hearts.
> **We have heard of God's miracles in other times;**
> **our ancestors have kept the story alive for us.**
Give ear, all people, to God's word for today.
Taste the bounty of God's blessing here and now.
> **We long for a faith that makes sense for today.**
> **We want to keep the story alive for new generations.**
God's revelation is for all people, near and far.
God is waiting to communicate with you and me.
> **May God have mercy on us and all people.**
> **Surely God's will shall be made known to us.**

Lavon Bayler, *Fresh Winds of the Spirit, Book 2:
Liturgical Resources for Year A* (Cleveland, Ohio: The Pilgrim
Press, 1992), 120. Used by permission.

Ainslie Roberts, *The Storyteller*, 1976, as reproduced in *Ainslie Roberts and the
Dreamtime* (Richmond, Victoria, South Australia: J.M. Dent Pty, 1988).
Used by permission.

**Go with God,
telling your story
to all who
will hear it.**

Interview

with an Older Family Member or Friend

The people of the Bible understood the importance of sharing their stories. In fact, much of the Bible was written to "tell to the coming generation the glorious deeds of God." Passing on stories from one generation to another is an important act in our families, community of faith, and neighborhood as well.

Choose

an older relative or friend and arrange a time to meet for an "interview." Let the person you have chosen know that you want to hear a story of an event that was important in his or her own life, or how a world event (such as a war) affected his or her life.

When you meet with the person, be sure to take along a notebook and something to write with, or a cassette recorder and a blank cassette. After listening to the story, seek more information if the person you are talking with feels comfortable in answering the questions below or other questions that you have prepared.

who? where? when? what? how?

- What was happening to you?

- How did you feel about it at the time?

- How do you feel about the event as you look back on it now?

- What was the reaction of the people around you?

- How old were you when this happened?

- What style of clothing did you wear then?

- What kind of transportation did you use?

- How was life different than it is now?

- What role do you think God played in this event?

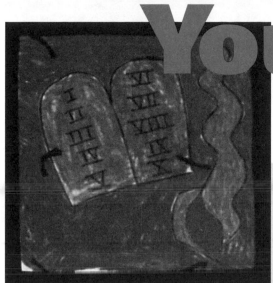

You Shall...

I am the Sovereign your God, who brought you out of the land of Egypt, out of the house of slavery; you shall have no other gods before me.

Exodus 20:2–3

These two images are taken from a quilt.

- **Which image are you drawn to first?**
- **Which one tells you more?**
- **What do the Ten Commandments mean in your life?**

Grade 4 at St. Francis Xavier School, Moses Quilt, details, 1994, 45 West High Street, Gettysburg, PA 17325. Used by permission.

Instructions for the Ten Commandments Game (game on reverse side)

This game can be played by you at home. Just reinterpret the questions (which are written for a group of youth) to fit your personal situation. Be sure to notice that each question corresponds to one of the **Ten Commandments** (printed toward the center of the board game).

Toss a coin to determine how many spaces to move your marker (a button) on the game board: heads = 2 spaces, tails = 1 space.

Write the response to the question on a piece of paper. The result of your responses to the questions your button lands on will be a covenant between you and God as to how you wish to live your life.

The Ten Commandments Game

Decide how you will sign this covenant (signatures, thumbprints, picture symbols, etc.).

Why is it important to honor your parents?

Do you speak respectfully about your parents? How can you do this if you are angry with them?

What can you do to keep your Sabbath holy?

How many Sundays a month can you commit to coming to church?

Decide what color markers to use for your final draft of this covenant.

What is the difference between "kill" and "murder"?

Honor your father and mother.

Remember the Sabbath day and keep it holy.

What are some appropriate ways to use God's name?

Create a group consensus statement about your feelings toward capital punishment.

You shall not murder.

You shall not make wrongful use of God's name.

What does it mean to "make wrongful use" of God's name?

What is the definition of "adultery"?

What nonvisual symbols or actions can you have or do each week to remind you of God's presence?

How is it possible to commit adultery with your thoughts?

You shall not commit adultery.

You shall not make for yourself an idol of God.

What symbols for God do you have in your gathering space? Are they appropriate symbols or are they idols?

Is taking something that won't be missed stealing?

You shall not steal.

You shall have no other gods before me.

Do you worship other gods, such as money, clothes, or possessions? How will you pay more attention to God?

Talk about respect for other people's property.

You shall not bear false witness against your neighbor.

You shall not covet anything that belongs to your neighbor.

How will you acknowledge God's presence each week when you meet together?

Decide on a title for your covenant.

Is it okay to lie to protect your best friend?

What would the consequences be if you were caught lying to protect your best friend?

What does "covet" mean? Why is it considered a sin?

Why isn't it okay to want something that belongs to someone else, even if you don't tell anyone or do anything about it?

START

18

Many Called, Few Chosen

Jesus said, "The dominion of heaven may be compared to a king who gave a wedding banquet for his son. He sent his slaves to call those who had been invited to the wedding banquet, but they would not come. For many are called, but few are chosen."

Matthew 22:2–3, 14

Rembrandt Harmensz van Rijn, *The Parable of the Unworthy Wedding Guest*, detail, The Albertina Museum, Vienna, Austria. Used by permission.

How did the unworthy guest fail to meet God's expectations?

What colors would you add to this drawing?

Benediction Litany
(from Philippians 4:4–9)

Leader:
Rejoice in God always; again I will say, Rejoice!

Learners:
We will go from here rejoicing!

Leader:
And the peace of God, which surpasses all understanding, will guard your hearts and minds in Christ Jesus.

Right: Whatever is true,

Left: Whatever is honorable,

Right: Whatever is just,

Left: Whatever is pure,

Right: Whatever is pleasing,

Left: Whatever is commendable.

Leader:
If there is anything worthy of praise, think about these things. And the God of peace will be with you.

Learners:
And the God of peace will be with you.

Leader:
Go in peace.

All: Amen.

Most of us look forward to being asked to go to a party or to go out to a movie with friends. These kinds of gatherings are usually a lot of fun. We expect them to include much laughter, some joking around, and a good supply of junk food! What would you expect a banquet hosted by God to be like?

CHANGE

Wait for me, Lord: I'm coming!
    Wait for me, Lord: I'm getting dressed!

I am clothing my eyes with goodness
    to look at everyone in friendship.

I am clothing my hands with peace
    to forgive without keeping track.

I am clothing my lips with a smile
    to offer joy all day long.

I am clothing my body and my heart
    with prayer to turn towards you,
    Lord whom I love.

Now I am ready!
It's me! Do you recognize me?
I have put on my best clothing!

Charles Singer, *Gospel Prayers* (Portland, Ore.: OCP Publications, 1992), 43. Used by permission of Editions du Signe.

What kinds of attitudes and behaviors do you think God expects you to "wear" to a party thrown by God?

BELONGING TO GOD

Jesus said, "Show me the coin used for the tax." And they brought him a denarius. Then Jesus said to them, "Whose head is this, and whose title?" They answered, "The emperor's." Then Jesus said to them, "Give therefore to the emperor the things that are the emperor's, and to God the things that are God's." When they heard this, they were amazed.

Matthew 22:19–22a

Titian, *The Tribute Money*, The National Gallery, London, England. Used by permission.

What do you see in this painting?

What do you think is happening here?

Which character intrigues you more by how he is depicted?

The artist entitled this *The Tribute Money*. Read Matthew 22:15—22 to find out why.

entrapment (en-trap'-ment) *n.* 1. The condition of being caught as in a trap. 2. The act of luring one into danger, difficulty, or self-incrimination.

WORLD'S HIGHEST STANDARD OF LIVING

There's no way like the American Way

Margaret Bourke-White, *Flood Victims, Louisville, Kentucky*, 1938, from "Margaret Bourke-White," *American Photo* 5, no. 4 (July/August 1994), 70–71. Used by permission of Time-Life Syndication,

What does the way you use money say about your relationship with God?

What would Jesus say to you about your use of money?

[God] coined us
in [God's] image. . . .
We are [God's] money,
and we should be spent. . . .
Money should circulate,
we should circulate;
money should go from hand to hand,
we should go from hand to hand; . . .
money should be used,
we should be used; . . .
money is going to be worn,
we should be going to be worn.

We should be spent,
we are coins,
God is trying to use us,
to pay off our debts,
to pay off the debts we owe each other
here on earth. . . .

Let us risk being used,
and we will be increased,
and the end will be glory. . . .

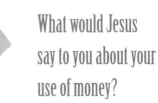

Joseph G. Donders, *Jesus the Stranger: Reflections on the Gospel* (Maryknoll, N.Y.: Orbis Books, 1978). Used by permission of Joseph G. Donders.

At Home with God

God, you have been our dwelling place in all generations. Before the mountains were brought forth, or ever you had formed the earth and the world, from everlasting to everlasting you are God.

Psalm 90:1–2

Charles E. Burchfield, *Six O'Clock*, Everson Museum of Art, Syracuse, N.Y. Used by permission.

Contract

I, _____ [your full name], promise with the help and guidance of God to make a better dwelling place or home with God for myself by doing the following this week:

_____

_____

_____

_____

This is signed by me in the presence of these witnesses

on this _____ day of _____, 199___, in the year of our God.

_____   _____   _____
[your signature]   [signature of your leader]   [signature of another youth]

You Are Mine

Words and music: David Haas, 1991

1 I will come to you in the si - lence,
2 I am hope for all who are hope - less,
3 I am strength for all the des - pair - ing,
4 am the Word that leads all to free - dom,

I will lift you from all your fear.
I am eyes for all who long to see. In the
heal - ing for the ones who dwell in shame.
am the peace the world can - not give.

You will hear my voice, I claim you as my choice, be
sha - dows of the night, I will be your light,
All the blind will see, the lame will all run free, and
I will call your name, em - brac - ing all your pain, stand

still and know I am here. *to st. 2*
come and rest in me. *to Refrain*
all will know my name. *to Refrain*
up, now walk, and live! *to Refrain*

Refrain

Do not be a - fraid, I am with you. I have called you each by name.

Come and fol - low me, I will bring you home; I

love you and you are mine. 4 I mine.

O God, Our Help of Ages Past

O God, our help in ages
    past,
our hope for years to come,
Our shelter from the
    stormy blast,
and our eternal home:

Under the shadow of your
    throne
your saints have dwelt
    secure;
Sufficient is your arm alone,
and our defense is sure.

...

O God, our help in ages past,
our hope for years to come,
Still be our God while
    troubles last,
and our eternal home!

Isaac Watts, in *The New Century Hymnal* (Cleveland, Ohio: The Pilgrim Press, 1995), 25.

This hymn based on Psalm 90 was written by Isaac Watts in 1719.

Home is where

no one ever forgets your name. Home is where no matter what you have done, you will be confronted, forgiven, and accepted. Home is where there is always a place for you at the table and where you can be certain that what is on the table will be shared. To be part of a home or a household is to have access to life.

M. Douglas Meeks, "Love and the Hope for a Just Society," in Frederick B. Burnham, Charles McCoy, and M. Douglas Meeks, *Love: The Foundation in the Theology of Jürgen Moltmann and Elisabeth Moltmann-Wendel* (San Francisco: Harper and Row, 1988), 44–45.

FROM TABLE TO TOWN

Some wandered in desert wastes, finding no way to an inhabited town; hungry and thirsty, their soul fainted within them. Then they cried to God in their trouble, and God delivered them from their distress. And there God lets the hungry live, and they establish a town to live in.

Psalm 107:4–6, 36

WHAT DO YOU THINK THE WORDS "TABLE" AND "TOWN" HAVE TO DO WITH THIS PICTURE?

Manuscript illumination, *Depiction of a Medieval Town (August: Corn Harvest)*, c. 1500, *Goif Book of Hours*, MS. 24098, f.25v., British Library, London, England (Bridgeman/Art Resource, N.Y.). Used by permission

PSALM 107 LITANY

One: O give thanks to God, for God is good;

All: God's steadfast love endures forever.

One: Let those saved by God say,

All: God's steadfast love endures forever.

One: When we wander in desert wastes,

All: God's steadfast love endures forever.

One: When we are hungry and thirsty,

All: God's steadfast love endures forever.

One: When we are in trouble and call for God's help,

All: God's steadfast love endures forever.

One: God will continue to take us by the hand and bring us safely to those who will love us, because . . .

All: God's steadfast love endures forever. Amen.

God Is Good

MAKE AN ORIGAMI FISH

1. Fold a square piece of paper down the center at EF as shown in Figure 1, crease, and then unfold.

2. Bring forward corners A and B until they meet along the center line EF, forming Figure 2.

3. Fold at GH and IJ so that the edges KC and LD meet at the center line EF, as shown in Figure 3.

4. Fold upward at MN so that HJ meets point E as in Figure 4.

5. Pick up the paper and spread the two flaps HJ and GEI so that point M can be pushed up between them and extended as far as the center line EF. See Figures 4, 5, and 6. Do the same with point N. The result will be Figure 7.

6. Fold down the front flap at PQ in order to get Figure 8.

7. Bend forward points P and Q so that they meet at F (Figure 9).

8. Turn over and draw an eye as in Figure 10.

Florence Sakade, *Origami: Japanese Paper-folding, Book 1* (Rutland, Vt./ Tokyo, Japan: Charles E. Tuttle Company, 1957), 24–25. Used by permission.

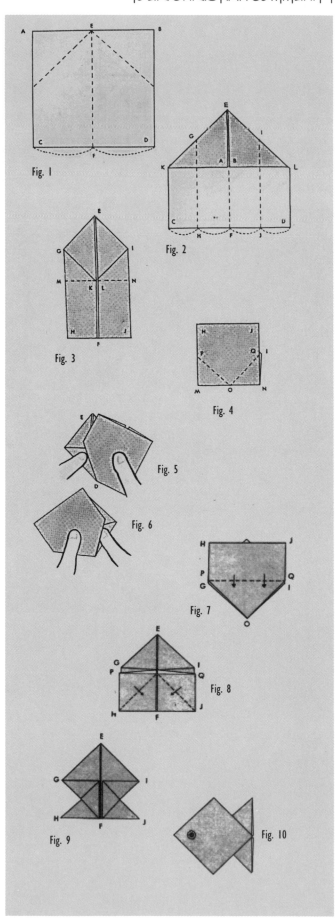

Fig. 1

Fig. 2

Fig. 3

Fig. 4

Fig. 5

Fig. 6

Fig. 7

Fig. 8

Fig. 9

Fig. 10

Choose This Day

Synthia Saint James, *Visions*, Los Angeles, California. Used by permission.

Joshua said, "Now if you are unwilling to serve God, choose this day whom you will serve, whether the gods your ancestors served in the region beyond the River or the gods of the Amorites in whose land you are living; but as for me and my household, we will serve God."

Joshua 24:15

The Road Not Taken

I shall be telling this with a sigh,

somewhere ages and ages hence;

two roads diverged in a wood, and I,

I took the one less traveled by,

and that has made all the difference.

Robert Frost, excerpt, in *New England Anthology of Robert Frost's Poems* (New York: Washington Square Press, 1971), 223. Used by permission.

Which road have you chosen?

Which road will you choose?

Whom do you serve?

The Story of Chung-Ming Kao: One Who Chose God

"Thirteen years ago," said the Rev. Chung-Ming Kao, former general secretary of the [Presbyterian Church in Taiwan], "I helped a human rights leader by offering him shelter. He was safe with us for four weeks, and then they discovered him and put him in prison. Not long after I was imprisoned for protecting him.

"At first, people were afraid for me and the church. They said, 'If your general secretary is in prison, your members will go to other churches and your church will soon close down.'

"I said, 'No, the church belongs to Jesus Christ, not to me. I knew that we had to be faithful. We added more than 40,000 new members during that most difficult time. I thank you for your prayers. I was in prison four years, three months and 21 days. In prison, I suffered very much, but God protected us all and confirmed that [God] is the living [God]."

In Mission 1994/1995: A Calendar of Prayer for the United Church of Christ (June 19, 1994) published by the United Church Board for Homeland Ministries and the United Chruch Board for World Ministries, Cleveland, Ohio. Used by permission.

This is one of the many poems Rev. Chung-Ming Kao wrote from his prison cell:

I asked the Lord for a bunch of fresh flowers
but instead he gave me an ugly cactus
with many thorns.
I asked the Lord for some beautiful butterflies
but instead he gave me many ugly
and dreadful worms.
I was threatened,
I was disappointed,
I mourned.
But after many days,
Suddenly,
I saw the cactus bloomed
with many beautiful flowers,
And those worms
became beautiful butterflies
flying in the Spring wind.
God's way is the best way.

In Mission 1994/1995: A Calendar of Prayer for the United Church of Christ (June 19, 1994) published by the United Church Board for Homeland Ministries and the United Chruch Board for World Ministries, Cleveland, Ohio. Used by permission.

"Whom Do You Serve?" Survey

In the boxes provided, write how you serve each of the persons listed at the top during each of the situations listed on the left. Then put a number in the corner of the three boxes that are the most important in your life, 1 being the most important, 2 the next important, and so on.

	God	Parents	Yourself	Your Friends
At Home	*Example: Give thanks at evening meal.*			
At School (or Work)				
With Friends				
During Favorite Activity				
At Church				

The Wise and Foolish Girls

MATTHEW 25

Jesus must have joined in many happy weddings when he was a boy. The bride and her friends would wait at her home for the bridegroom to come and get her. But no one knew when he would come. It might even be in the middle of the night! At last they would hear the shout—'The bridegroom is on his way!' And soon he would arrive, followed by a procession of excited people. Then all who were invited would return to the bridegroom's house for a week of feasting and celebration.

Jesus longed for people to follow him and come into his kingdom while they had the chance. He knew he would not be with them much longer. But a day was going to come when he would return to earth as king, in glory and power. It would be too late then for people to change their minds and choose to follow him.

'On that day,' Jesus told them, 'the kingdom of God will be like a wedding. Once there were ten girls who were waiting to join the bridegroom's procession. It was evening, so all had their lamps ready. But five of them had not taken any oil to burn. Night came on and all the girls slept.

'Suddenly at midnight, a cry rang out in the quiet street—"The bridegroom is on his way!"

'The girls started up and began to turn up their lamps. Then the five foolish ones realized their mistake. "We haven't any oil!" they wailed. "Please lend us some!" But the five wise girls had only enough for their own lamps. "We can't help you," they said, "go and buy some."

'While the five foolish girls were away, the bridegroom arrived. The five wise girls joined the procession and soon they were all safely inside the bridegroom's house. The door was shut.

'It was some time later when the five foolish girls came knocking on the door.

According to Ability

Jesus said, "For it is as if someone, going on a journey, summoned slaves and entrusted property to them; giving to one five talents, to another two, to another one, all according to their ability; and went away. After a long time the master of those slaves came and settled accounts with them."

Matthew 25:14–15, 19

Glen Strock, *Parable of the Talents*, detail, Dixon, N.M. Used by permission of the artist.

Discover Your God-given Talents

In most cases, the things we enjoy doing most are the things we do the best. Follow the instructions below to determine what you enjoy doing the most. See if what you come up with is what you do best.

1 List at least three (but not more than ten) things you like to do with people:

_____

_____

_____

_____

2 List at least three (but not more than ten) things you like to do with objects or ideas:

_____

_____

_____

_____

3 Rank all of the responses from #1 and #2 in order of preference, the first one being the one you enjoy the most.

4 Now underline all of the responses that you feel you really do well.

5 From the underlined items, circle the one(s) that you feel God gave you the ability to accomplish.

6 Give thanks to God for your gifts and abilities.

This picture includes symbols of Antonio Lomas' life and talents. Try to identify his talents by looking at the symbols that represent them. You may want to note your findings in the space below.

Carmen Lomas Garza, *Ofrendo para Antonio Lomas* (Offering to Antonio Lomas), San Francisco, California. Used by permission.

We Offer Our Talents

One: Why have you come to this sacred space?

All: *We have come to offer symbols of the gifts and talents God has entrusted to us.*

One: What will you do with these talents when you go forth from this place?

All: *We will use them in service to others so that God's domain of love, justice, and peace may fill the earth. Amen.*

30

The Least of
These

"Truly I tell you, just as you did it to one of the least of these who are members of my family, you did it to me."

Matthew 25:40b

Aaron Douglas, *The Judgment Day*, as reproduced in James Weldon Johnson, *God's Trombones: Seven Negro Sermons in Verse* (New York: Viking Press, 1927). Used by permission of Viking Penguin, a division of Penguin Books USA, Inc.

The sound of the trumpet signals the coming of the risen Christ to judge the earth. Read Jesus' description of this judgment in Matthew 25:31–46. Also look at *The Judgment Day* painting. Reflect on these questions.

How does the painting suggest that "all nations will be gathered before" the risen Christ?

Suppose the trumpet were to sound right now. Where would you put yourself in this painting? Why?

If you were to paint this scene, how would you do it? What colors would you use? How would you draw the figures?

Mona Reeder, *Hau Li Eating Lunch*, as reproduced in *The Daily Republic*, Suisun City, CA, The Best of Photojournalism. Used by permission.

Finding it difficult to adjust to his new school in a new country, Hau Li often eats by himself at Crescent Elementary School.

Bobby Cory Comes Home, as reproduced in *The Year in Pictures*, National Press Photographers Association, University of Missouri School of Journalism, 1993. Used by permission.

Thirty-six-year-old Bobby Cory, who has AIDS, comes home to Wichita and support.

O God, who is old, and lives on fifty dollars a month, in one crummy room and can't get outside,
Help us to see you.

O God, who is fifteen and in the sixth grade,
Help us to see you.

O God, who is three and whose belly aches in hunger,
Help us to see you, as you have seen us in Jesus Christ our Lord.

O God, who sleeps in a bed with your four brothers and sisters, and who cries and no one hears you,
Help us to touch you.

O God, who has no place to sleep tonight except an abandoned car, an alley or deserted building,
Help us to touch you.

O God, who is uneducated, unskilled, unwanted, and unemployed,
Help us to touch you, as you have touched us in Jesus Christ our Lord.

. . .

O God, who is chased by the cops, who sits in jail for seven months with no charges brought, waiting for the Grand Jury and no money for bail,
Help us to know you.

. . .

O God, who is unorganized, and without strength to change your world, your city, your neighborhood,
Help us to join you.

O God, who is fed up with it all and who is determined to do something, who is organizing people for power to change the world,
Help us to join you, as you have joined us in Jesus Christ our Lord. Amen.

Robert W. Castle, Jr., "As You Did It to One of the Least of These My Brethren," in *The Wideness of God's Mercy*, ed. Jeffrey W. Rowthorn (Minneapolis: Seabury Press, 1985), 2:164–65. Used by permission.

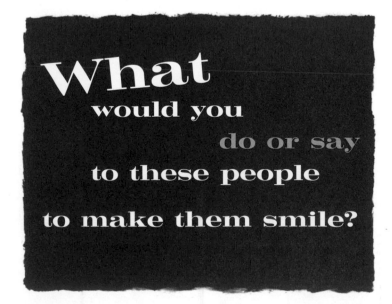

What would you do or say to these people to make them smile?

KEEP AWAKE

"Therefore, keep awake—
for you do not know when
the owner of the house
will come, in the evening,
or at midnight, or at cockcrow,
or at dawn, or else the owner
may find you asleep when
coming suddenly. And what
I say to you I say to all:
Keep awake."

Mark 13:35–37

Claudio Jiminez, *Festival Cross*, detail. Photograph by Dr. LaFarge.
Used by permission of que tenaga Buena Mano, P.O. Box 762,
Santa Fe NM 87504, 505-982-2912.

Prayer for Lighting the Advent Candle

O God who promises much to your people, we enter this season of Advent with anticipation and expectancy. We light the first candle this morning to represent the ways in which you awaken us to the promise of your coming into our lives. We ask you to walk with us in the days ahead so that we can be awakened to the meaning of your coming and prepared to receive you. **Amen.**

KEEP AWAKE,
BE ALWAYS READY

Words: Arthur G. Clyde, 1993

Tune: WACHET AUF, by Philipp Nicolai, 1599

1 Keep a - wake, be al - ways rea - dy, God's time ap - proach - es
2 Rise and shine for One is com - ing whose love will quench all

sure and stea - dy, God's strength will keep your heart from blame.
na - ture's thirst - ing to be made whole for - ev - er more.

Clouds, the Spir - it's light con - ceal - ing, dis - perse, God's pur - est
On that day to end all weep - ing, death's swords trans - formed to

light re - veal - ing; cre - a - tion will its Sov - ereign name. Dry
tools of reap - ing, the God of might will mer - cy pour. In -

branch - es burst forth green, God's ad - vent signs are
car - nate, God ap - pears em - brac - ing all our

seen: Hal - le - lu - jah! Christ's judg - ment won, God's
tears: Hal - le - lu - jah! God's maj - es - ty e -

will be done; God's new do - min - ion thus be - gun.
ter - nal - ly re - vealed to set the cos - mos free.

Words Copyright © 1993 by The Pilgrim Press. Used by permission.

Salvador Dali, *Girl Standing at the Window*, 1925, Museo d'Arts Contemporanea, Madrid, Spain (Bridgeman/Art Resource, N.Y.). Used by permission.

Keep Awake !
for you do not know when Jesus will come.

Get READY

"See, I am sending my messenger ahead of you, who will prepare your way; the voice of one crying out in the wilderness: 'Prepare the way of the Sovereign, make straight the Sovereign's paths.'"

Mark 1:2b–3

Diego Rivera, *The Offering*, 1923–28, Secretaría de Educacion Publica, Court of Fiestas, Level 1, South Wall, Mexico City, Mexico (Schalkwijk/Art Resource, N.Y.). Reproduccion autorizada por el instituto Nacional de Bellas Artes y Literatura. Used by permission.

What are some ways that people prepare for the arrival of Jesus?

PRAYER FOR LIGHTING THE ADVENT CANDLE

God who comes into our lives in the flesh, we again light the first candle, which symbolizes the ways you awaken us to your presence. As we light another candle on this second Sunday of Advent, show us how to prepare our hearts for your arrival. Change us, O God, that we may be the people you call us to be.
AMEN.

THINGS I WILL DO TO PREPARE FOR CHRISTMAS

★   ★   ★   ★   ★

"Prepare the way of the Sovereign." —Mark 1:3

DEC.

1 _____
_____

2 _____
_____

3 _____
_____

4 _____
_____

5 _____
_____

6 _____
_____

7 _____
_____

8 _____
_____

9 _____
_____

10 _____
_____

11 _____
_____

12 _____
_____

13 _____
_____

14 _____
_____

15 _____
_____

16 _____
_____

17 _____
_____

18 _____
_____

19 _____
_____

20 _____
_____

21 _____
_____

22 _____
_____

23 _____
_____

24 _____
_____

25 Christmas
_____

GET READY

Good News Coming

For as the earth brings forth its shoots, and as a garden causes what is sown in it to spring up, so the Sovereign God will cause righteousness and praise to spring up before all nations

Isaiah 61:11

Prayer for Lighting the Advent Candle

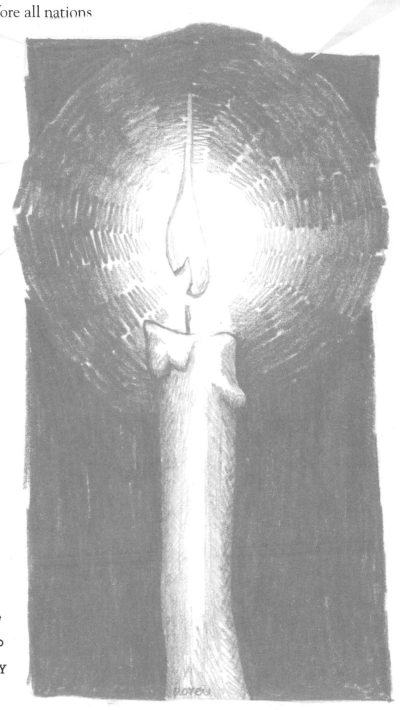

God whose coming into the world causes us to rejoice, we have lighted candles symbolizing the ways in which you awaken and prepare us for the miracle of Christ entering the world. We gather today and light a third candle. This candle reminds us of the celebration and great joy we experience because of all that you do in our lives and in the world. We long to be filled with the joy that you have in store for us in the future when Christ returns to gather the whole human family as one. Amen.

Piet Mondrian, *Red Amaryllis with Blue Background*, c. 1907, water color, 18 3/8 x 13″, Sydney and Harriet Janis Collection, The Museum of Modern Art, New York, N.Y. Photograph © 1996, The Museum of Modern Art. Used by permission.

Spring Song

the green of Jesus

is breaking the ground

and the sweet

smell of delicious Jesus

is opening the house and

the dance of Jesus music

has hold of the air and

the world is turning

in the body of Jesus and

the future is possible

Lucille Clifton, in *Good Woman: Poems and a Memoir 1969–1980* (Brockport, N.Y.: BOA Editions, Ltd., 1987). Used by permission.

For as the earth brings forth its shoots . . . God will cause righteousness and praise to spring up.

Isaiah 61:11

GREETINGS Favored One!

Henry O. Tanner, *The Annunciation*, 1898, W. P. Wilstach Collection, The Philadelphia Museum of Art, Philadelphia, Pa. Used by permission.

The angel Gabriel came to Mary and said, "Greetings, favored one! God is with you." But she was much perplexed by the words and pondered what sort of greeting this might be. The angel said to her, "Do not be afraid, Mary, for you have found favor with God. And now, you will conceive in your womb and bear a son, and you will name him Jesus."

Luke 1:28–31

Prayer for Lighting the Advent Candle

Holy One, who acts in our lives in mysterious ways, we have lighted candles that remind us to awaken, prepare, and celebrate your coming. Today we light a fourth candle, which represents your invitation to us to explore the mysteries of your actions in our lives and in the world. We seek your guidance as we continue to explore all that you are and all that you do among us through Jesus Christ whom you sent. Amen.

The Magnificat

And Mary said,
My soul magnifies God,
    and my spirit rejoices in God
        my Savior,
for God has looked with favor on
        the lowliness of God's
        servant.
        Surely, from now on all
        generations will call
        me blessed;
for the Mighty One has done
        great things for me,
    and holy is God's name.
God's mercy is for those who fear
        God
        from generation to generation.
God has shown strength with
        God's arm;
        God has scattered the proud in the
        thoughts of their hearts.
God has brought down the
        powerful from their
        thrones,
    and lifted up the lowly;
God has filled the hungry with
        good things,
    and sent the rich away empty.
God has helped God's servant Israel
        in remembrance of God's mercy,
according to the promise God made
        to our ancestors,
    to Abraham and to his
        descendants forever.

Luke 1:46–55

Ethan Hubbard, *Young Woman of Costura, Guatemala*, as reproduced in Ethan Hubbard, *Straight to the Heart: Children of the World* (Chelsea, Vt.: Craftsbury Common Books, 1992). Used by permission of the photographer.

Dear Cousin Elizabeth,
Something mysterious happened to me today. I was in my room when suddenly . . .

the WISE Ones

It had been revealed to Simeon by the Holy Spirit that he would not see death before he had seen God's Messiah. There was also a prophet, Anna. She was of a great age. She came, and began to praise God and to speak about the child to all who were looking for the redemption of Jerusalem.

Luke 2:26, 36a, 38

Song of SIMEON

Holy One, now let your servant go in peace;

your word has been fulfilled:

my own eyes have seen the salvation

which you have prepared in the sight of every people:

A light to reveal you to the nations

and the glory of your people Israel.

Luke 2:29–32, translated by the International Consultation on English Texts, 1975

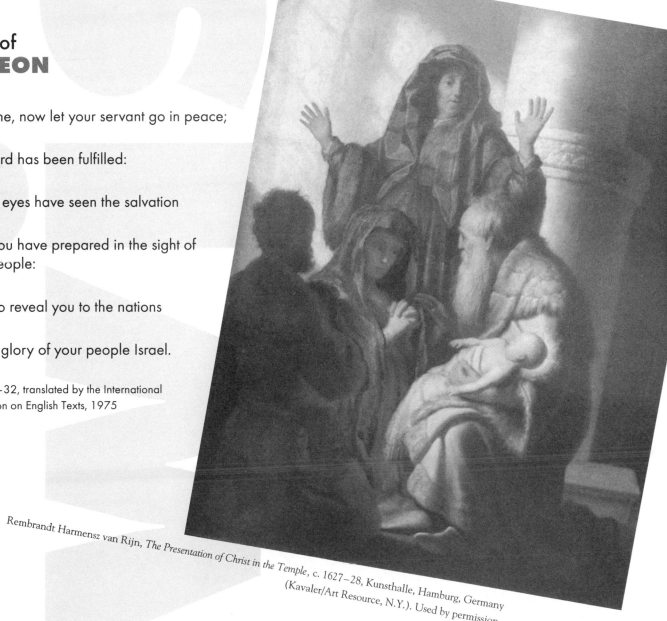

Rembrandt Harmensz van Rijn, *The Presentation of Christ in the Temple,* c. 1627–28, Kunsthalle, Hamburg, Germany (Kavaler/Art Resource, N.Y.). Used by permission.

Prayer for Lighting the Christmas Candle

Holy One, who in glory and majesty came to us in the form of a gentle child, we greet you this new morning. In watchfulness we have lighted candles that symbolize your efforts to awaken and prepare us for this joyous moment. We have lighted candles to symbolize the celebration we anticipate at your coming and your invitation to us to explore the mystery of your incarnation. Today we gather and light the center Christ candle, asking that you will use it and us to help the world recognize your presence among us. We pray that all may recognize your grace at work in us and see that our faith in you leads to wisdom and insight, through Jesus Christ the Messiah. Amen.

MENTORS
or Wise Ones in Your Own Life

☞ Who has played a major role in helping you formulate your goals for your life?

☞ Who has helped you recognize and develop your talents?

☞ Who do you look to for guidance? Why?

☞ How do you respond or react to the wisdom and insight this person has given you?

Michael Freeman, *Shaker Woman*, London, England.
Used by permission.

Child
Full of Grace

John Giuliani, *Hopi Mother and Child*, Bridge Building Images,
P.O. Box 1048, Burlington VT 05402. Used by permission.

And from the fullness of the Child have we all received, grace upon grace. For the law was given through Moses; grace and truth came through Jesus Christ. No one has ever seen God; the only Child, who is in the bosom of God the Mother and Father, that one has made God known.

John 1:16–18

Toda la Tierra
(All Earth Is Waiting)

Dice el profeta al pueblo de Israel:
"De madre virgen ya viene Emmanuel,"
será "Dios con nosotros," hermano será,
con él la esperanza al mundo volverá.

Thus says the prophet to those of Israel,
"A virgin mother will bear Emmanuel":
One whose name is "God with us," our Savior shall be,
through whom hope will blossom once more within our hearts.

Alberto Taulè, *Toda la Tierra (All Earth Is Waiting)*, trans. Gertrude C. Suppe, in *The New Century Hymnal* (Cleveland: Pilgrim Press, 1995). Words Copyright © 1993 Centrode Pastoral Liturgica. Administered by OCP Publications, 5536 NE Hassolo, Portland OR 97213. All rights reserved. English translation Copyright © 1989 The United Methodist Publishing House. Used by permission.

**As [human] alone,
Jesus could not have saved us;
as God alone he would not.
Incarnate, he could and did.**

Malcolm Muggeridge, *Jesus*, as quoted in
The Harper Religious and Inspirational Quotation Companion,
comp. and ed. Margaret Pepper (New York:
Harper and Row, 1989), 254.

John 1:14, 16—18

NEW REVISED STANDARD VERSION	NEW INTERNATIONAL VERSION	NEW JERUSALEM BIBLE	CONTEMPORARY ENGLISH VERSION
14 And the Word became flesh and lived among us, and we have seen his glory, the glory as of a father's only son, full of grace and truth. . . . 16 From his fullness we have all received, grace upon grace. 17 The law indeed was given through Moses; grace and truth came through Jesus Christ. 18 No one has ever seen God. It is God the only Son, who is close to the Father's heart, who has made him known.	14 The Word became flesh and made his dwelling among us. We have seen his glory, the glory of the One and Only, who came from the Father, full of grace and truth. . . . 16 From the fullness of his grace we have all received one blessing after another. 17 For the law was given through Moses; grace and truth came through Jesus Christ. 18 No one has ever seen God, but God the One and Only, who is at the Father's side, has made him known.	14 The Word became flesh, he lived among us, and we saw his glory, the glory that he has from the Father as the only Son of the Father, full of grace and truth. . . . 16 Indeed, from his fullness we have, all of us, received— one gift replacing another, 17 for the Law was given through Moses, grace and truth have come through Jesus Christ. 18 No one has ever seen God; it is the only Son, who is close to the Father's heart, who has made him known.	14 The Word became a human being and lived here with us We saw his true glory, the glory of the only Son of the Father. From him all the kindness and all the truth of God have come down to us. . . . 16 Because of all that the Son is, we have been given one blessing after another. 17 The Law was given by Moses, but Jesus Christ brought us undeserved kindness and truth. 18 No one has ever seen God. The only Son, who is truly God and is closest to the Father, has shown us what God is like.

What insights do these translations give you about who Jesus was?

What do they tell you about why Jesus came to earth?

What difference does Christ's coming to earth in the flesh (incarnation) to pour out God's grace upon humanity make in your own life?

You Are My Beloved

Just as Jesus was coming up out of the water, he saw the heavens torn apart and the Spirit descending like a dove on him. And a voice came from heaven, "You are my Child, the Beloved; with you I am well pleased."

Mark 1:10–11

The one who created us is waiting for our response to the love that gave us our being. God not only says: "You are my Beloved." God also asks: "Do you love me?" **and offers us countless chances to say** "Yes."

Henri Nouwen,
Life of the Beloved:
Spiritual Living in a Secular
World (New York: Crossroad,
1993), 106.

In what ways do you say "Yes!" to God?

John August Swanson, *The River*, serigraph © 1987, Los Angeles, California. Used by permission.

45

renewal

Baptism is the sacrament through which we are united to Jesus Christ and given a part in Christ's ministry. Baptism is the visible sign of an invisible event: the reconciliation of people to God. It shows the death of self and the rising to a life of obedience and praise. It shows also the pouring out of the Holy Spirit on those whom God has chosen. In baptism, God works in us the power of forgiveness, the renewal of the Spirit, and the knowledge of the call to be God's people always.

United Church of Christ Book of Worship (New York: United Church of Christ Office for Church Life and Leadership, 1986), 135–36. Used by permission.

What Ruler Wades through Murky Streams

1. What ruler wades through murky streams
   and bows beneath the wave,
   ignoring how the world esteems
   the powerful and brave?

   Refrain
   Water, River, Spirit, Grace,
   sweep over me, sweep over me!
   Recarve the depths your fingers traced
   in sculpting me.

2. Christ gleams with water brown with clay
   from land the prophets trod.
   Above while heaven's clouds give way
   descends the dove of God.

   Refrain

3. Come bow beneath the flowing wave.
   Christ stands here at your side
   and raises you as from the grave
   God raised the crucified.

   Refrain

Thomas H. Troeger. Words Copyright © 1984; rev. 1993, Oxford University Press, Inc. Used by permission.

Here I Am!

Now God came and stood there, calling as before, "Samuel! Samuel!" And Samuel said, "Speak, for your servant is listening."

1 Samuel 3:10

Listen, my child, with the ear of your heart. Hearken to my words if you would have life!

St. Benedict, sixth century

What might God want to whisper into the ear of a young person today?

Matthew Inglis, *Walls Have Ears*, 1990, as reproduced in Bill Hare, *Contemporary Painting in Scotland* (East Roseville, New South Wales, Australia: Craftsmen House, 1990). Photograph by Ralph Hughes. Used by permission of Craftsmen House.

Matthew Inglis created a humorous, free-standing sculpture with gigantic ears that literally grow out of the walls. Who do you suppose is listening? Who is talking?

Thuma Mina

Send Me Now

South African traditional song

Leader 1 Thu - ma mi - na.

All
1 Thu - ma mi - na, thu - ma mi - na,
1 Send me, Je - sus, send me, Je - sus,
2 Lead me, Je - sus, lead me, Je - sus,
3 Fill me, Je - sus, fill me, Je - sus,

Thu - ma mi - na, So - man - dla.
Send me, Je - sus, send me now.
Lead me, Je - sus, lead me now.
Fill me, Je - sus, fill me

Leader
1 Send me now.
2 Lead me now.
3 Fill me now.
now.

Copyright © 1984 by Walton Music Corporation. Used by permission.

The Word to Jonah

The word of God
came to Jonah a second time,
saying, "Get up, go to
Nineveh, that great city, and
proclaim to it the
message that I tell you."

Jonah 3:1–2

Howard Finster, *Nineveh (Garden Wall)*, Summerville, Georgia.
Used by permission of Finster Folk Art.

Folk artist and preacher Rev. Howard Finster
celebrates the primary relationship with God
and humanity in Paradise Garden, his two-and-a-half acre
backyard creation. It was built from broken parts of bicycles, cars,
machines, and tools as a message of hope to mend a broken world. On a wall
Finster portrays the repentant Ninevites from the story in the book of Jonah.

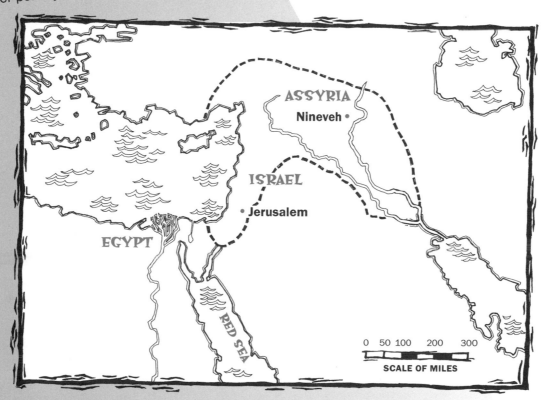

The Assyrian Empire (circa 750 B.C.E.)

Thuma Mina
Send Me Now

Thuma mina.
Thuma mina, thuma mina,
Thuma mina, Somandla.

Send me now.
Send me, Jesus, send me, Jesus,
Send me, Jesus, send me now.

Lead me now.
Lead me, Jesus, lead me, Jesus,
Lead me, Jesus, lead me now.

Fill me now.
Fill me, Jesus, fill me, Jesus,
Fill me, Jesus, fill me now.

Ways you can hear God's call to witness in _____:

(your city or town)

1. _____ 2. _____

3. _____ 4. _____

5. _____

"Fish Story"

Joel is fishing on a lake in Alaska at night and suddenly imagines his rabbi from home in New York is with him. He feels a big tug on line.

Rabbi Schulman: I wouldn't do that if I were you, Joel. I don't think we want to lose our connection with what's down there. We could be on to something big.

Joel: Something big? What do you mean? Big like how? You think . . .

Rabbi Schulman: He—She—whose name may not be uttered.

Joel: You mean God? You think God's on the other end of this line?

Rabbi Schulman: Fish imagery is very big throughout the Judeo-Christian canon: Jonah, the miracle of the loaves and the fishes, the earliest sign of Christianity, in fact,—before the cross even, was the fish. . . .

Later, in the whale . . .

Rabbi Schulman: We're inside, Joel.

Joel: Inside what?

Rabbi Schulman: The fish . . . the belly of the beast. . . . You know, Jonah may be the key here.

Joel: Key to what?

Rabbi Schulman: The meaning of all this. Think a minute, Joel. Why was Jonah swallowed in the first place? [God] told him to go to Nineveh, cry out against their wickedness. Instead, Jonah flees, hops a boat for Tarshish. [God] raises a ruckus, Jonah gets the heave ho. What's the message, Joel?

Joel: Next time go to Nineveh.

Rabbi Schulman: Responsibility. Jonah was trying to avoid his responsibility.

Jeff Melvoin, "Fish Story," excerpts from *Northern Exposure*, episode 18, pp. 45, 46–47, 1993. Pipeline Productions, Inc., Cold Water Canyon Avenue, Studio City CA 91604.

A New teaching

They were all amazed, and they kept on asking one another, "What is this? A new teaching—with authority! Jesus commands even the unclean spirits, and they obey him."

Mark 1:27

Edvard Munch, *The Scream*, Nasjonalgalleriet, Oslo, Norway.
Used by permission.

Jesus Has Authority

Read Mark 1:21–28.
Pretend you are the unclean spirit who spoke to Jesus. Perhaps you are speaking as the unseen spirit who cries out in *The Scream*, as illustrated in this art.

What are you saying to Jesus that is not recorded in the Bible?

Try to explain to the crowd how Jesus has authority over you.

Silence, Frenzied, Unclean Spirit

A 1. "Silence, frenzied, unclean spirit!"
   cried God's healing Holy One.

B Cease your ranting!

C Flesh can't bear it;

D flee as night before the sun."

E At Christ's words the demon trembled,
   from its victim madly rushed,

F while the crowd that was assembled
   stood in wonder, stunned and hushed.

G 2. Lord, the demons still are thriving
   in the gray cells of the mind:

H tyrant voices,
   shrill and driving,

I twisted thoughts that grip and bind,

J doubts that stir the heart to panic,

K fears distorting reason's sight,

L guilt that makes our loving frantic,

M dreams that cloud the soul with fright.

N 3. Silence, Lord, the unclean spirit
   in our mind and in our heart;

O speak your word that
   when we hear it,
   all our demons shall depart.

P Clear our thought

Q and calm our feeling;

R still the fractured, warring soul.

S By the power of your healing
   make us faithful, true, and whole.

Thomas H. Troeger, in *The United Methodist Hymnal*
(Nashville: The United Methodist Publishing House, 1989),
264. Used by permission of Oxford University Press.

Linda Post, *Solstice*, R. Michelson Galleries, Northampton, Mass.
Used by permission of R. Michelson Galleries.

Go, healed, with the authority of Jesus!

What fears in your life will you give Jesus authority over?

What doubts do you want Jesus to cast out of your mind?

What feelings within your "fractured, warring soul" do you want Jesus to take authority over and heal?

With Wings like Eagles

Ayako Araki, *Migrating Birds*, as reproduced in *The Bible Through Asian Eyes* ed. Masao Takenaka and Ron O' Grady (Auckland, New Zealand: Pace Publishing in association with the Asian Christian Art Association, 1991), 71. Used by permission of the Asian Christian Art Association.

God gives power
to the faint,
and strengthens
the powerless.
Even youths will
faint and be weary,
and the young
will fall exhausted;
but those who wait
for God shall renew
their strength,
they shall mount up
with wings like eagles,
they shall run and
not be weary, they shall
walk and not faint.

Isaiah 40:29–31

In circumstances where those in the best condition possible to humans *stumble and collapse...*, a special group runs on with new and greater vigor than before. They are *those waiting [hoping] on [God]...*. Here the ideas overlap: "waiting hope" or "hopeful waiting." Israel's impatience and insistence on prompt action from God could become [their] undoing. An attitude which can wait for the God of the ages and [God's] plan will gain *strength* to *rise* above the moment, *not tire* and *not faint*, but go on and on. The figure of the eagle's wings is apt. The soaring eagle is borne aloft not by his powerful wings, but by the wind's currents lifting his rigid pinions. Those *waiting* are those prepared to be lifted and carried aloft by the Spirit of God in [God's] time and [God's] way.

You are to me, **O God, what wings are to the bird.**

Hindu prayer, in *Prayers, Praises, and Thanksgivings* (New York: Dial Books, 1992). Used by permission.

John D. W. Watts, *Isaiah 34–66* (Waco, Tx.: Word Books, 1987), 95–96.

Psalm
147:1–11

1 Praise God!

  For it is good to sing praises to our God;

  for God is gracious, and a song of praise is seemly.

2 God builds up Jerusalem,

  and gathers the outcast of Israel,

3 heals the brokenhearted,

  and binds up their wounds.

4 determines the number of the stars,

  and gives to all of them their names.

5 Great is our God, and abundant in power,

  with understanding beyond measure.

6 God lifts up the downtrodden,

  and casts the wicked to the ground.

7 Sing to God with thanksgiving;

  make melody upon the lyre to our God,

8 who covers the heavens with clouds,

  prepares rain for the earth,

  and makes grass grow upon the hills,

9 who gives to the beasts their food,

  and to the young ravens which cry!

10 God does not delight in the strength of the horse,

  nor take pleasure in the might of a human being;

11 but God takes pleasure in those who fear God,

  in those who hope in God's steadfast love.

Inclusive-Language Psalms: From an Inclusive-Language Lectionary
(New York: The Pilgrim Press, 1987), 137. Used by permission.

Cliff Bahnimptewa, *Kwahu (Eagle)*,
The Heard Museum, Phoenix, AZ.
Used by permission.

Closing Prayer

Today, God, help me let go of my

need to do it alone and my belief

that I am alone. Help me to tap

into Your Divine Power and

Presence, and Your resources for

love, help, and support that's there

for me. Help me know I am loved.

Melanie Beattie, *The Language of Letting Go*
(New York: HarperCollins, 1990), 6.
Used by permission.

Clothed with joy

You have turned my mourning into dancing;
you have taken off my sackcloth and clothed
me with joy, so that my soul may praise you
and not be silent. O Sovereign my God,
I will give thanks to you forever.

Psalm 30:11–12

Psalm 26

When the day comes on which our victory
will shine like a torch in the night,
it will be like a dream.
We will laugh and sing for joy.
Then the other nations will say about us,
"The Lord did great things for them."
Indeed, [God] is doing great things for us;
That is why we are happy in our suffering.

Lord, break the chains of humiliation and death,
just as on that glorious morning
when you were raised.
Let those who weep as they sow
the seed of justice and freedom
gather the harvest of peace
and reconciliation.

Those who weep as they go out
as instruments of your love
will come back singing for joy,
as the witness to the disappearance of hate
and the manifestation of love in your world.

Zephania Kameeta, "Psalm 26,"
in *Why, O Lord?*
(Geneva: World Council
of Churches, 1986).
Used by permission.

*Women of Namibia
Dancing* (Afrapix/
Impact Visuals, N.Y.).
Used by permission.

A dance of joy and empowerment
inspires the women of Namibia
to keep up their fight for full
freedom for women of their country.

Psalm 30

1 I will extol you, O God, for you
  have drawn me up,
      and did not let my foes rejoice
      over me.

2 O God my God, I cried to you for help
      and you have healed me.

3 O God, you brought up my soul from Sheol,
      restored me to life from among
      those gone down to the Pit.

4 Sing praises to God, O you God's
  faithful ones,
      and give thanks to God's holy name. R

5 For God's anger is but for a moment;
  God's favor is for a lifetime.
      Weeping may linger for the night,
      but joy comes with the morning.

6 As for me, I said in my prosperity,
      "I shall never be moved."

7 By your favor, O God, you had
  established me as a strong mountain;
      you hid your face; I was dismayed.

8 To you, O God, I cried,
      and to you I made supplication: R

9 "What profit is there in my death, if I
  go down to the Pit?
      Will the dust praise you? Will it
      tell of your faithfulness?

10 "Hear, O God, and be gracious to me!
      O God, be my helper!"

11 You have turned my mourning into dancing;
      you have taken off my sackcloth
      and clothed me with joy,

12 so that my soul may praise you and
  not be silent.
      O God, my God, I will give thanks
      to you forever. R

I Will Do a NEW Thing

Do not remember the former things, or consider the things of old. I am about to do a new thing; now it springs forth, do you not perceive it? I will make a way in the wilderness and rivers in the desert.

Isaiah 43:18–19

Wilhelm Morgner, *Fields*, 1912, Museum Bochum, Bochum, Germany. Used by permission.

IMAGINE this painting of a landscape in wild, vivid colors. The artist painted it in colors usually not seen in nature—a new way of viewing the world.

What are the advantages to seeing your world and God's world in new ways?

I am about to do a new thing; now it springs forth, do you not see it?

What new thing is God doing in your life right now?

My Personal Timeline of
God's Creating Presence in My Life

Directions: At the top line, write your birthdate. Make marks across the line to show approximate dates and events in your life when you were aware of God's creating and renewing presence. Write a few words about each event at the date you have marked.

LITANY of Thanksgiving for
God's Creating and Renewing Presence

One: Behold: the ripples of fire
buried deep in the dark, rich ground.

All: We are here.
We bring our memories and legacy.
We bring our bamboo and rice.
We bring our taro and palm.
We bring our earth and ocean.

One: Behold: the first shoots that burst out
from the ground and reach toward the sun.

All: We are here.
We bring our struggles and hopes.
We bring our shovels and picks
to this land of opportunity.
We bring our irons and ditches
to this land of promise.
We bring our broken hands and weeping hearts
to this land of milk and honey.

One: Behold: the golden flower that blooms with all the beauty
and the power and fragrance of almighty God!

All: We are not yet here,
but we are coming.
Help us, O God,
to open our minds,
to open our hearts,
to open our spirits
to the bright, new potential you have given us
in each moment of life.

One: We thank you, O God.

All: We thank you, O God. Amen.

Adapted from Alpha D. Goto, "A Litany of Memory and Potential,"
United Church of Christ Book of Worship (Cleveland, Ohio: United Church
of Christ Office for Church Life and Leadership, 1986), 547.
Used by permission of the author.

2003

As Jesus sat at dinner in Levi's house, many tax collectors and sinners were also sitting with Jesus and the disciples—for there were many who followed him. When the scribes of the Pharisees saw that he was eating with sinners and tax collectors, they said to the disciples, "Why does Jesus eat with tax collectors and sinners?" When Jesus heard this, he said to them, "Those who are well have no need of a physician, but those who are sick; I have come to call not the righteous but sinners."

Mark 2:15–17

John Perceval, *Christ Dining in Young and Jackson's,* 1947, collection of Helen and Maurice Alther, Melbourne, Australia. Used by permission of the artist.

**What would it be like to eat
with the group gathered in this painting?**

Levi's House

People of God

People of God,
look about and see the faces of those
we know and love—
neighbors and friends,
sisters and brothers—
a community of kindred hearts.

People of God,
look about and see the faces
of those we hardly know—
strangers, sojourners, forgotten friends,
the ones who need an outstretched hand.

Ann Asper Wilson, excerpt, *United Church of Christ Book of Worship* (Cleveland, Ohio: United Church of Christ Office of Church Life and Leadership, 1977). Used by permission.

Spirit, unite us, make us, by grace . . . loving the whole human race.

We Are Your People

Words: Brian Wren, 1973; rev. 1993

Music: John Wilson, 1973

We are your peo - ple: Spir - it of grace,
Joined in com - mu - ni - ty, trea - sured and fed,
Rich in di - ver - si - ty, help us to live
Glad of tra - di - tion, help us to see
Give, as we ven - ture jus - tice and care
Spir - it, u - nite us, make us, by grace,

you dare to make us Christ to our neigh - bors
may we dis - cov - er gifts in each oth - er,
clos - er than neigh - bors, o - pen to strang - ers,
in all life's chang - ing, where Christ is lead - ing,
(peace - ful, in - sist - ing, risk - ing, re - sist - ing),
will - ing and read - y, Christ's liv - ing bod - y,

of ev - ery cul - ture and place.
will - ing to lead and be led.
a - ble to clash and for - give.
where our best ef - forts should be.
wis - dom to know when and where.
lov - ing the whole hu - man race.

Upon a High Mountain

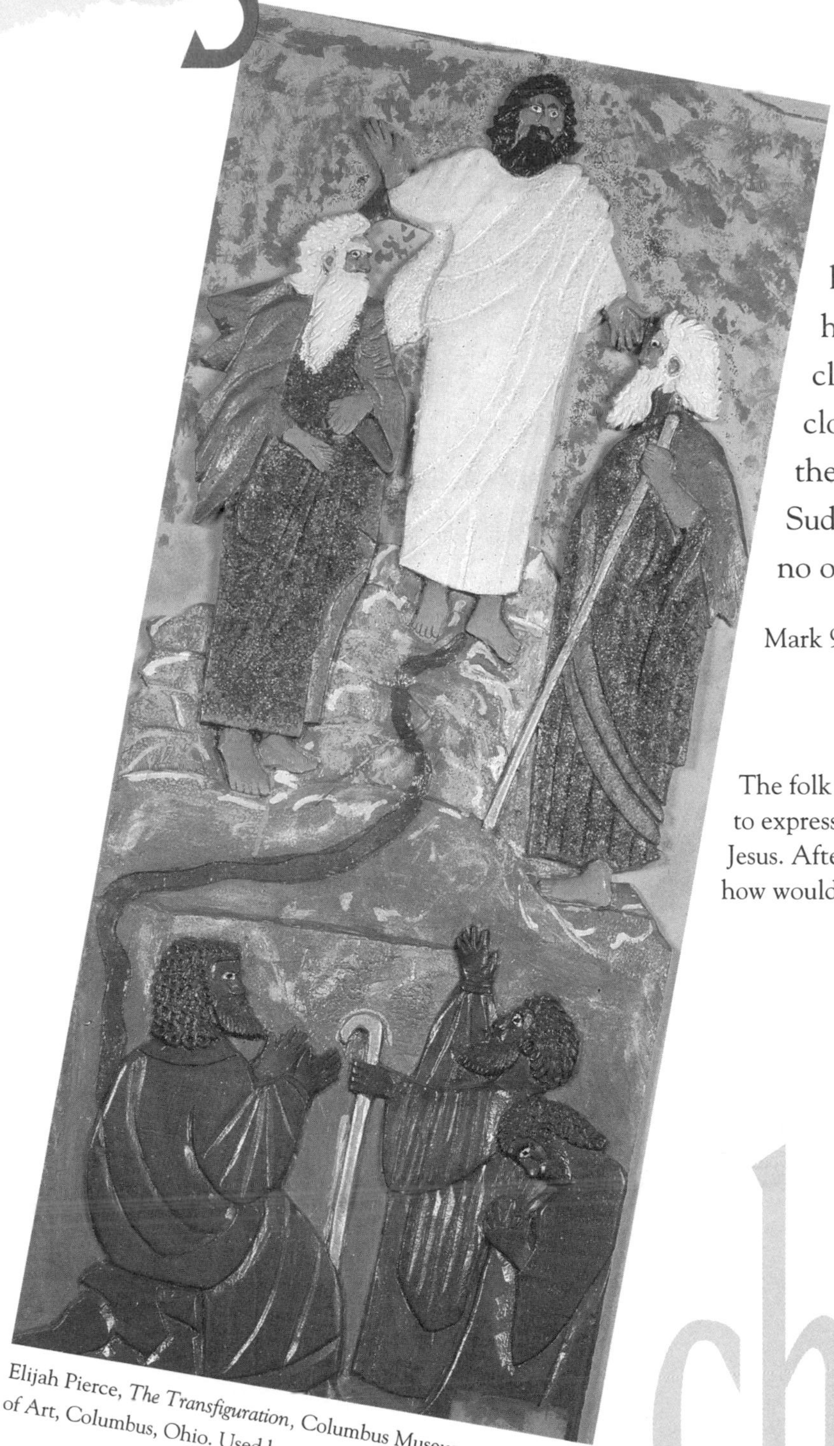

Six days later, Jesus took with him Peter and James and John, and led them up a high mountain apart, by themselves. And he was transfigured before them. Then a cloud overshadowed them, and from the cloud there came a voice, "This is my Child, the Beloved; to this one you shall listen!" Suddenly when they looked around, they saw no one with them anymore, but only Jesus.

Mark 9:2, 7–8

Elijah Pierce, *The Transfiguration*, Columbus Museum of Art, Columbus, Ohio. Used by permission.

The folk artist Elijah Pierce cut and painted wood to express a moment in the transfiguration of Jesus. After climbing up and down the mountain, how would you describe the Transfiguration?

We're climbin' up the mountain.
We will be changed.
We're climbin' step by step.
We will be changed.
We're at the top and Jesus shines!
We will be changed.
We're makin' it down the mountain.
We will be changed.
We're here in Jerusalem!
We will be changed.
We will be transfigured—
Changed.

changed

61

All he said when he got up close to her was "Follow me," and she bounded down to his side with all the bob and speed of one so old. . . . They walked along in deep silence for a long time. Finally she started telling him about how many years she had cooked for them, cleaned for them, nursed them. . . . She told him indignantly about how they had grabbed her when she was singing in her head and not looking, and how they had tossed her out of his church. . . . A old heifer like me, she said, straightening up next to Jesus, breathing hard. But he smiled down at her and she felt better instantly and time just seemed to fly by. When they passed her house, forlorn and sagging, weatherbeaten and patched, by the side of the road, she did not even notice it, she was so happy to be out walking along the highway with Jesus.

She broke the silence once more to tell Jesus how glad she was that he had come . . . and how she never expected to see him down here in person. Jesus gave her one of his beautiful smiles and they walked on. She did not know where they were going; someplace wonderful, she suspected. The ground was like clouds under their feet, and she felt she could walk forever without becoming the least bit tired. She even began to sing out loud some of the old spirituals she loved, but she didn't want to annoy Jesus, who looked so thoughtful, so she quieted down. They walked on, looking straight over the treetops into the sky, and the smiles that played over her dry wind-cracked face were first clean ripples across a stagnant pond. On they walked without stopping.

Alice Walker, "The Welcome Table," in *In Love and Trouble: Stories of Black Women* (New York: Harcourt, Brace and Co., 1970), 43. Used by permission.

HOW do you picture the Transfiguration?

Read Mark 9:2–9. In the space below, draw the scene of the Transfiguration as you envision it. Put yourself on the mountain as a reminder that an encounter with Jesus, God's Beloved, is a transforming experience.

God said, "I establish my covenant with you, that never again shall all flesh be cut off by the waters of a flood, and never again shall there be a flood to destroy the earth." God said, "This is the sign of the covenant that I make between me and you and every living creature that is with you, for all future generations: I have set my bow in the clouds, and it shall be a sign of the covenant between me and the earth."

Genesis 9:11–13

God's Rainbow PROMISE

When it **rains,**
I feel . . .

....
....
....
....

When the **sun** is **shining,**
I feel . . .

....
....
....
....

When I see **a rainbow,**
I feel . . .

....
....
....
....

God our light,

make your Church like a **rainbow**

shining and **proclaiming** *to all the world*

that the storm is at an end,

there is peace *for those who seek it*

and **love** for the **forgiving**.

Merciful God,

grant to your faithful people *pardon* and *peace;*

that we may be cleansed from all our sins

and **serve you** with a *quiet* mind;

through Jesus Christ our Redeemer.

Make a Rainbow

To make a rainbow, you will need a flashlight, a glass full of
water, and a dark room. Place the flashlight so that you can
turn your back to it. Hold the glass in your left hand at about
45 degrees from the forward direction. You may not see a
rainbow right away, but by moving the glass slightly—lifting,
turning, and tilting—you will see red near the right-hand edge
of the glass. You have made a rainbow! (If you use several
glasses on a table, you can make all the colors of the rainbow.)

As you make this rainbow, the sign of God's covenant promise
with you and with every creature of the earth, **remember and
celebrate God's everlasting commitment to you.**

God's Covenant, in *Vienna Genesis*, Cod. Theol. Graec 31, page 5,
Austrian National Library, Vienna, Austria.
Used by permission.

An Everlasting Covenant

I will make you exceedingly fruitful; and I will make nations of you, and rulers shall come from you. I will establish my covenant between me and you, and your offspring after you throughout their generations, for an everlasting covenant, to be God to you and to your offspring after you.

Genesis 17:6–7

Sarai
Sarah

Abram
Abraham

God is a promise-maker . . .

Sarai, unable to have children (Genesis 16:1), sends her slave Hagar to be Abram's wife (Genesis 16:3).

Hagar bears Ishmael (Genesis 16:15).

Abram is 99; God promises that he will be "ancestor of a multitude of nations"; God changes his name to Abraham (Genesis 17:4–5).

Sarai is 90; God promises that she will "give rise to nations"; God changes her name to Sarah (Genesis 17:15–16).

Abraham and Sarah laugh about God's promise (Genesis 17:17, 18:12).

Sarah gives birth to Isaac (Genesis 21:2–3).

. . . and a promise-keeper.

Film still from *The Color Purple*, © 1985, Warner Brothers, Inc. Photo provided by Photofest, New York, N.Y. Used by permission.

Me and you must never part.
Me and you must have one heart.
Ain't no ocean, ain't no sea,
Keep my sister away from me.
Me and you must never part,
Me and you must have one heart.

The Color Purple, book by Alice Walker, screenplay by Menno Meyjes. Program content, artwork, and photography © 1985 Warner Bros., Inc. Used by permission.

O Thou who art the Light of the minds that know thee,
the Life of the souls that love thee,
and the Strength of the thoughts that seek thee;
help us so to know thee, that we may truly love thee,
so to love thee that we may fully serve thee,
whose service is perfect freedom; through Jesus Christ our Lord. Amen.

Gelasian Sacramentary, as quoted in *Prayers for Services*, ed. Morgan Phelps Noyes (New York: Charles Scribner's Sons, 1934), 115. Used by permission.

Over turn the Tables

In the temple Jesus found people selling cattle, sheep, and doves, and the money changers seated at their tables. He poured out the coins of the money changers and overturned their tables. Jesus told those who sold the doves, "Take these things out of here! Stop making God's house a marketplace!"

John 2:14, 15b–16

Read **John** 2:13–22.

How did Jesus' action show a commitment to God?

How does Jesus' action free people from unfairness?

What does Jesus' action show his followers about how to live?

El Greco, *Cleansing the Temple*, detail, 1584–94, National Gallery, London, England. Used by permission.

Committed to **Righteous** Living

Photo by LeRoy Calbom. Used by permission of the United Church Board For World Ministries

We sniff glue because we need to. We steal—watches, necklaces. We don't have anything to eat, we **don't have** anywhere to sleep, we don't have anywhere to stay—that's why we steal. I steal, I walk around. I sniff glue, and then I can't do **anything**. I have eight brothers and sisters and I can't really stay at home, so I live on the street. That's how I lead my life. I'd like all of us to be healthy and have a house to live in. We should all have our rights, we should have our hope and our family alive. We shouldn't need this death squad to kill people, we shouldn't need to rob or steal.

World in Action as quoted in Gilberto Dimenstein, *Brazil: War on Children* (Latin American Bureau, 1991), 22–23.

Righteousness is . . .

How is this boy's situation similar to those who were cheated in the Temple?

How might Jesus respond with righteousness to this boy and his circumstances?

Think about people you know or have read about who are treated unfairly. What injustices have they experienced?

How can you show your commitment to God by acting on behalf of those who are treated unfairly?

God So Loved

For God so loved the world
that God gave God's only Child,
so that everyone who believes
in that Child should not perish
but have eternal life.

John 3:16

"For God so loved the world..."

David Driskell,
West Window, 1990,
Peoples Congregational
United Church of Christ,
Washington, D.C.
Used by permission.

How do I respond **to God's great gift** of love?

Psalm 132

GOD GAVE GOD'S ONLY CHILD

Jesus is love

because God is love

Jesus is love

because God so loved the world

    that Jesus was sent in love

    for love

    Jesus is love

    breaks open the eternal possibility

    for love

    to be for all

because Jesus is love.

Benjamin F. Chavis, *Psalms from Prison*
(Cleveland, Ohio: The Pilgrim Press, 1994),
149. Used by permission.

The Spirit of the Living God

May the Spirit of the Living God . . .

Be above you to bless you,

    Before you to guide you,

Behind you to forgive you,

    Beside you to comfort you,

Beneath you to sustain you,

    and continually surprise you with

great love for you each moment

    along life's way.

Robert G. Kemper,
in Betty Jane and
J. Martin Bailey,
Youth Plan Worship
(New York: The
Pilgrim Press, 1987),
195. Used by permission.

The best way to know God

is to love many things.

—Vincent van Gogh

Nada te Turbe
Nothing Can Trouble

Words and music: The Taizé Community, 1991

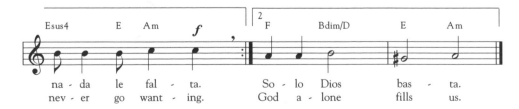

Na - da   te   tur - be,   na - da   te es - pan - te.   Quien a   Dios   tie - ne
Noth- ing   can   trou - ble,   noth- ing   can   fright - en.   Those who seek God shall

na - da   le   fal - ta.   So - lo   Dios   bas - ta.
nev - er   go   want - ing.   God   a - lone   fills   us.

The Law Within

I will put my
law within them,
and I will write
it on their hearts;
and I will be
their God, and
they shall be
my people.

Jeremiah 31:33b

Marc Chagall, *Klageleid des Jeremias*, 1956, © ARS, New York, N.Y.
Used by permission of ARS.

When I consider what is **important** to me,
what does it **reveal** about
my relationship with God?

My teachings are easy to understand
and easy to put into practice.
Yet your intellect will never grasp them,
and if you try to practice them, you'll fail.

My teachings are older than the world.
How can you grasp their meaning?

If you want to know me,
look inside your heart.

Tao Te Ching: A New English Version, foreword and notes
by Stephen Mitchell (New York: HarperPerennial, 1988), 70.
Translation copyright © 1988 by Stephen Mitchell. Used by
permission of HarperCollins Publishers, Inc.

God Be in My Head

God be in my head, and in my understanding;

God be in my eyes, and in my looking;

God be in my mouth, and in my speaking;

God be in my heart, and in my thinking;

God be at my end, and my departing.

From *Sarum Primer* (1558), in Betty Jane and J. Martin Bailey,
Youth Plan Worship (New York: The Pilgrim Press, 1987), 195.

Nada te Turbe
Nothing Can Trouble

Words and music: The Taizé Community, 1991

Na-da te tur- be, na-da te es-pan- te. Quien a Dios tie - ne
Noth-ing can trou-ble, noth-ing can fright - en. Those who seek God shall

na-da le fal- ta. So-lo Dios bas - ta.
nev-er go want-ing. God a-lone fills us.

Betty LaDuke, *Guatemala: Procession*, Ashland, Oregon. Used by permission.

Then those who went ahead and those who followed were shouting, "Hosanna! Blessed is the one who comes in the name of God! Blessed is the coming dominion of our ancestor David! Hosanna in the highest heaven!" Then Jesus entered Jerusalem and went into the temple.

Mark 11:9–11a

Jerusalem

The calendar below lists the scripture readings that describe the daily events in Jesus' life between Palm Sunday and Easter, along with a symbolic action you can do to remember Jesus each day. Can you think of other things to do? If so, add them to each entry. Also add at least one activity to the "to do" list that you would normally do each day.

SUNDAY: Celebrate   Read Mark 11:1–11.

Celebrate Jesus' entry into my life.

To do:

MONDAY: Cleanse   Read Mark 11:12–19.

"Clean out" a negative thought today.

To do:

TUESDAY: Teach   Read Mark 11:20–13:37.

Teach someone something about Jesus today.

To do:

WEDNESDAY: Anoint   Read Mark 14:1–11.

Praise someone today.

To do:

THURSDAY: Last Supper and Arrest   Read Mark 14:12–72.

Say grace at every meal today.

To do:

FRIDAY: Death   Read Mark 15:1–47.

Pray for those who mourn today.

To do:

SATURDAY: Sabbath   Read Philippians 2:5–11.

Observe one minute of silence today.

To do:

SUNDAY: Resurrection   Read Mark 16:1–20.

Think about how the resurrected Christ is present in your own life.

To do:

This is a holy week.

Jesus is *Risen!*

As they entered the tomb, the women saw a youth, dressed in a white robe, sitting on the right side; and they were alarmed. But the youth said to them, "Do not be alarmed; you are looking for Jesus of Nazareth, who was crucified. Jesus has been raised, and the body is not here. Look, there is the place they laid the body."

Mark 16:5–6

José Clemente Orozco, *The White House*, 1925–27, Instituto Nacional de Bellas Artes y Literatura, Mexico City, Mexico. Reproduccion autorizada por el instituto Nacional de Bellas Artes y Literatura. Used by permission.

How did the women in Mark 16:1–8 respond to the empty tomb?

What did they feel? **What** did they do?

How do you respond to the risen Christ?

Psalm 118:14–24

God is my strength and my song,

and has become my salvation.

Hark, glad songs of victory

in the tents of the righteous:

"The right hand of God does valiantly,

the right hand of God is exalted,

the right hand of God does valiantly!"

Hallelujah!

This is the day God has made.

I shall not die, but I shall live,

and recount the deeds of God.

God has chastened me sorely,

but has not given me over to death.

Hallelujah!

This is the day God has made.

Open to me the gates of righteousness,

that I may enter through them

and give thanks to God.

This is the gate of God;

the righteous shall enter through it.

Hallelujah!

This is the day God has made.

I thank you that you have answered me

and have become my salvation.

The stone which the builders rejected

has become the head of the corner.

Hallelujah!

This is the day God has made.

This is God's doing;

it is marvelous in our eyes.

This is the day which God has made;

let us rejoice and be glad in it.

Hallelujah!

This is the day God has made.

Inclusive Language Psalms: Readings for Years A, B, and C
(New York: The Pilgrim Press, 1987), 112. Used by permission.

God of terror and joy,

you arise to shake the earth.

Open our graves and give us

back the past;

so that all that has been buried

may be freed and forgiven,

and our lives may return to you

through the risen Christ, Amen.

Janet Morley, *All Desires Known: Prayers Uniting Faith and Feminism*
(Wilton, Conn.: Morehouse-Barlow, 1988), 16. Used by permission.

# of One Heart and Soul

Now the whole group of those who believed were of one heart and soul, and no one claimed private ownership of any possessions, but everything they owned was held in common. With great power the apostles gave their testimony to the resurrection of the Sovereign Jesus, and great grace was upon them all.

Acts 4:32–33

A Community of One Heart and One Soul...

The old folks used to slip out in the fields and thickets to have prayer meetings, and my mother always took me along for fear something would happen to me if left behind. They would all get around a kettle on their hands and knees and sing and pray and shout and cry. My mother was a great prayer, and she always asked God to take care of her son—meaning me. I would look and listen; sometimes I would cry. I don't know what I was crying for, but the meaning and singing was so stirring that I couldn't help it. Now, as I look back, I know that these things sunk deep in my heart. . . . All of my family were God-fearing, and I came up on an atmosphere charged with faith, hope, and the Holy Spirit. Outwardly we sang; inwardly we prayed.

"A Preacher from a God-fearing Plantation," in *God Struck Me Dead: Voices of Ex-Slaves*, ed. Clifton H. Johnson (Cleveland, Ohio: The Pilgrim Press, 1993), 69, 90. Used by permission.

Faith Ringgold, *Church Picnic*, painted story quilt, Englewood, New Jersey. Photo by Gamma I. Used by permission of the artist.

Paul describes several essential unifying factors of Christian community in Acts 2:42:

Fellowship

Pray

Meet Needs

How – does your church engage in these activities?
– are you involved?

Teach

Break Bread

Pieces

Pieces
A world in pieces
A life in pieces . . .

We want to live new times, Lord God.
We want to see flourishing signs of hope
that we may put the pieces together
and rebuild a united world.

We cry out for the Spirit of Unity,
so that from the four corners of the Earth
the breath of new life may caress all beings . . .

Come, Spirit of God,
spread over nations in conflict in former Yugoslavia,
spread over groups and factions in South Africa,
spread over gangs of Blacks and Hispanics in New York and L.A.,
spread over . . .

May a new wind blow
to fill us with desire and strength
so the pieces may become one body
the world's body
the people's body
because you created us as one, and that is how you want us to be.

Ernesto Barros Cardoso, "Pieces, Pieces, a world in pieces . . .," reprinted from
Poems, Prayers and Songs. Copyright 1993, EGGYS Working Group on Liturgy and Bible Studies,
Rio de Janeiro, Brazil, #20. Used by permission of the author.

Communities of faith are united in a variety of ways.

▶▶ How do the people pictured in *Church Picnic* seem to be united?

▶▶ How are the people in *"God Struck Me Dead"* united?

▶▶ How does "Pieces" express hope for unity?

You Are Witnesses

You are invited to tell the good news

Then Jesus opened their minds to understand the scriptures, and said to them, "Thus it is written, that the Messiah is to suffer and to rise from the dead on the third day, and that repentance and forgiveness of sins is to be proclaimed in the Messiah's name to all nations, beginning from Jerusalem. You are witnesses of these things."

Luke 24:45–48

R S V P

How would you tell the story of Jesus' resurrection to someone who had never heard it before?

What might these witnesses be saying to others about Jesus?

Osmond Watson, *Hallelujah*, 1969, The National Gallery of Jamaica, Kingston, Jamaica. Photo by Donnette Zacca. Used by permission.

Thuma Mina (Send Me Now)

South African traditional song

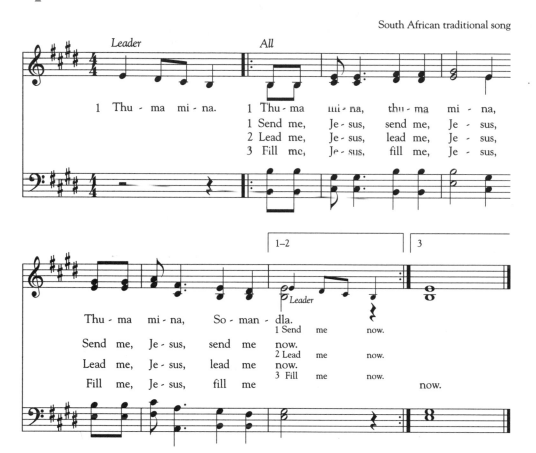

ACCEPT THE INVITATION

Jesus, we believe you; all we heard is true.

You break the bread, we recognize you,

you are the fire that burns within us,

use us to light the world.

A New Zealand Prayer Book (Auckland, New Zealand: William Collins Publishers, 1989), 595. Used by permission.

Let Us LOVE

We know love by this, that Jesus laid down life for us—and we ought to lay down our lives for one another. How does God's love abide in anyone who has the world's goods and sees a brother or sister in need and yet refuses to help? Little children, let us love, not in word or speech, but in truth and action.

1 John 3:16–18

Adam Kufeld, *Sixth Anniversary Commemoration of the Assassination of Archbishop Oscar Romero* (Impact Visuals, N.Y.). © Adam Kufeld, Impact Visuals. Used by permission.

Archbishop Oscar Romero, who is pictured on the sign behind the cross, served the people of El Salvador. His special concern for those who are very poor eventually cost him his life. He laid down his life for his friends, loving them in truth and action. In our scripture lesson for today from 1 John 3:16–24, we are called to love like this.

You can learn more about Archbishop Romero by renting the video *Romero,* a movie based on his life. The movie stars Raul Julia and was directed by John Duigan.

Leader:	Whom shall we love?
People:	***Our brothers and sisters in need.***
Leader:	How shall we love?
People:	***We shall lay down our lives for one another.***
Leader:	Why shall we love?
People:	***Because God has first loved us.***
All:	***Amen.***

As followers of Christ, we are called to love.

What is love?

LOVE is action!

START

Do a deed of love... advance **2** spaces.

Help a brother in need... advance two spaces.

Help a sister in need... advance **2** spaces.

Lay down your life for a friend... go straight to last space!

I John 3:18

Directions

Think of deeds that you can do to show your faith in action. Write these in the empty boxes. Flip a coin to begin. Heads allows you to move forward two spaces; tails lets you move forward one. When you reach the last box, look up 1 John 3:18 and write it in the space.

How does your life show God's love in action?

Abide in Me

Abide in me as I abide in you. Just as the branch cannot bear fruit by itself unless it abides in the vine, neither can you unless you abide in me. I am the vine, you are the branches. Those who abide in me and I in them bear much fruit, because apart from me you can do nothing.

John 15:4–5

How do plants live and grow? In part, they rely on roots for nourishment and strength. As Christians, our "roots" are in Christ. Through Christ we live and grow and bear fruit. The fruit we bear because of Christ is love.

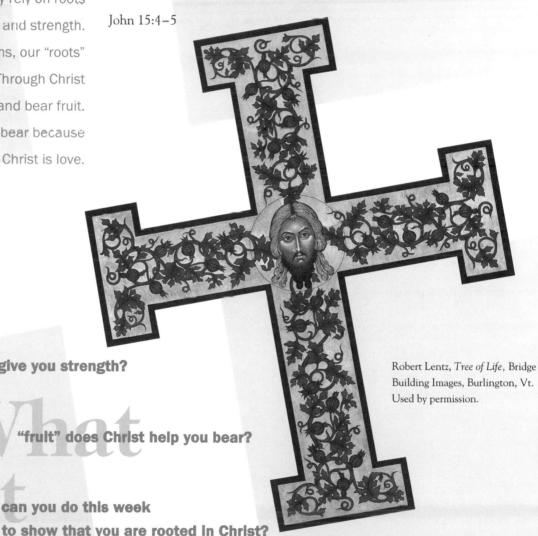

Robert Lentz, *Tree of Life*, Bridge Building Images, Burlington, Vt. Used by permission.

How does Christ give you strength?

What "fruit" does Christ help you bear?

What loving action can you do this week to show that you are rooted in Christ?

I am the vine . . .

So through you who are life

we will produce the fruit of life

if we choose to engraft ourselves into you.

And from what source,
O tree—
since of yourself you are dead and barren—
do you get these fruits of life?
From the tree of life—
for unless you are engrafted into him
you would have no power
to produce any fruit at all,
because you are nothing.

Catherine of Siena, "Prayer 17," in The Prayers of Catherine Siena, ed. Suzanne Noffke (New York: Paulist Press, 1983), 149. Used by permission.

One loving thing that I will do . . .

By being rooted in Christ I gain . . .

you
are
the
branches.

When Mahalia Sings

We used to gather at the high window
of the holiness church and, on tip-toe,
look in and laugh at the dresses, too small
on the ladies, and how wretched they all
looked—an old garage for a church, for pews,
old wooden chairs. It seemed a lame excuse
for a church. Not solemn or grand,
with no real robed choir, but a loose jazz band,
or so it sounded to our mocking ears.
So we responded to their hymns with jeers.

Sometimes those holiness people would dance,
and this we knew sprang from deep ignorance
of how to rightly worship God, who after
all was pleased not by such foolish laughter
but by the stiffly still hands in our church
where we saw no one jump or shout or lurch
or weep. We laughed to hear those holiness
rhythms making a church a song fest:
we heard this music as the road to sin,
down which they traveled toward that end.

I, since then, have heard the gospel singing
of one who says I worship with clapping
hands and my whole body, God, whom we must
thank for all this richness raised from dust.
Seeing her high-thrown head reminded
me of those holiness high-spirited,
who like angels, like saints, worshipped as whole
men with rhythm, with dance, with singing soul.
Since then, I've learned of my familiar God—
He finds no worship alien or odd.

Quandra Prettyman, in *I Am the Darker Brother:
An Anthology of Modern Poems by Negro Americans*
(New York: Macmillan, 1968), 56–57. Used by permission.

Sing a New Song!

O sing to God a new song. God has remembered God's steadfast love and faithfulness to the house of Israel. All the ends of the earth have seen the victory of our God.

Psalm 98:1a, 3

James Chapin, *Ruby Green Sings*, Norton Gallery of Art, West Palm Beach, Fla. Used by permission of the James Chapin Estate.

Amen

This day, God, help us to **sing and shout** for our love of you.

Psalm 98

O sing a new song to God who has done marvelous things.

Sing praises to God with the lyre.

With trumpets and the sound of the horn, make a joyful noise before God.

Let the sea roar and all that fills it.

Let the floods clap their hands; let the hills sing together for joy.

Read the portion of Psalm 98 above and answer the questions on the musical notes.

Why is the psalmist singing?

_____

_____

_____

_____

_____

What instruments does the psalmist mention?

_____

_____

_____

_____

_____

What other joyful noises are mentioned besides singing and playing instruments?

_____

_____

_____

_____

_____

What is the mood of this psalm?

_____

_____

_____

_____

_____

Music is an important part of life in many ways, but have you ever thought of music as an expression of your faith? Just as we can pray to God, we can sing to God too. If you wrote a song thanking God for the marvelous things in your life, what would it sound like? What instruments would you use? Would the song have any words? If so, what would they be?

That They May Be **One**

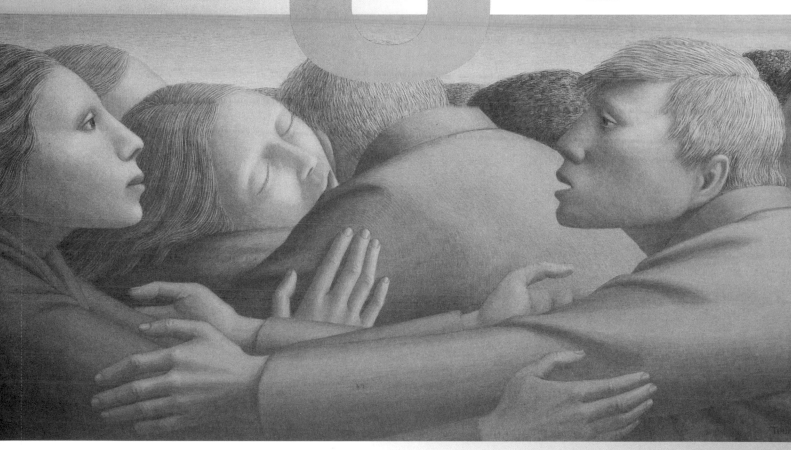

George Tooker, *Embrace of Peace*, Hartland, Vermont. Used by permission of the artist.

In what ways does your church reach out to bind the community together?

Jesus said, "I am no longer in the world, but they are in the world, and I am coming to you. Holy God, Father and Mother, protect them in your name that you have given me, so that they may be one, as we are one."

John 17:11

Before sharing the bread and wine, parishioners offer "greetings of peace," turning to each other and to those nearby to exchange a handshake or embrace. For Tooker, the embrace symbolizes the community he has found in the church, and the community he hopes to find in paradise. The painting is thus a visual rendering of heaven and earth where the sexes and races mix harmoniously. It is where "we should be."

Thomas H. Carver, *George Tooker* (New York: Marisa del Re Gallery, 1988), 3.

Living God,
Loving God,
You are the source
of all that is,
and all that is
is holy
when it seeks itself in You.
You are the bond
that unites us all
and erases all division.
May we be one
as You are one in us
and we in You.
Amen.

Miriam Therese Winter, *WomanWord:
A Feminist Lectionary and Psalter: Women of
the New Testament* (New York: Crossroad, 1990),
260. Used by permission.

Read

Look

Read John 17:11. Look at this picture of a sculpture. It portrays the cross used in the emblem of the United Church of Christ. It is based on the ancient Christian symbol known as the Cross of Victory. The crown on top of the cross signifies the reign of the risen Christ over all the world. The circle on which the cross is placed represents the world, the place where Christ's disciples are to witness. What do you see in this art that helps you to experience the oneness of God and Jesus and the church?

All May Be One, United Church of
Christ Headquarters, Cleveland, Ohio.
Used by permission.

Use this space to draw or describe in words what it means to be one.

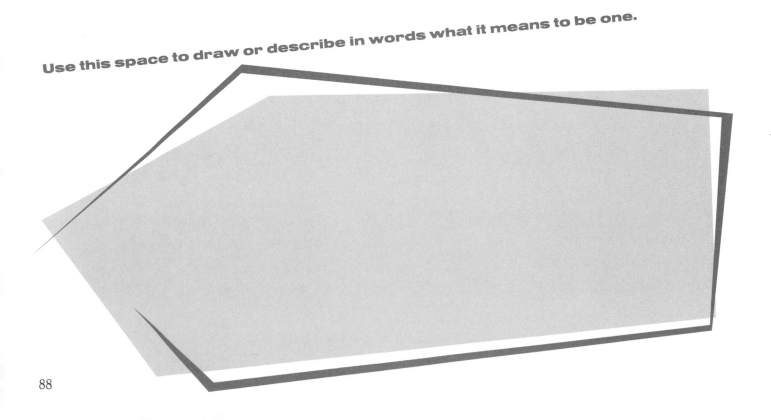

Spirit of Comfort

The Spirit helps us in our weakness; for we do not know how to pray as we ought, but that very Spirit intercedes with sighs too deep for words. And God, who searches the heart, knows what is the mind of the Spirit, because the Spirit intercedes for the saints according to the will of God.

Romans 8:26–27

How do the people in this picture feel the comforting presence of the Holy Spirit?

Beauford Delaney, *Can Fire in the Park*, 1946, National Museum of American Art, Washington D.C. (National Museum of American Art, Washington D.C./ Art Resource, N.Y.). Used by permission.

Come down, O Love divine,

Seek out this soul of mine

And visit it with Your own ardor glowing;

O Comforter, draw near, Within my heart appear,

And kindle it, Your holy flame bestowing.

Bianco da Siena, "Come Down, O Love Divine," trans. Richard Frederick Littledale, in *The Presbyterian Hymnal* (Louisville: Westminster/John Knox Press, 1990), 313. Used by permission.

O comforter

Footprints

One night a man had a dream. He dreamed he was walking along the beach with Christ. Across the sky flashed scenes from his life. For each scene, he noticed two sets of footprints in the sand: one belonging to him, and the other to Christ.

touch us

When the last scene of his life flashed before him, he looked back at the footprints in the sand. He noticed that many times along the path of his life there was only one set of footprints. He also noticed that it happened at the very lowest and saddest times in his life.

carry us

This really bothered him and he questioned Christ about it. "Christ, you said that once I decided to follow you, you'd walk with me all the way. But I have noticed that during the most troublesome times in my life, there is only one set of footprints. I don't understand why when I needed you most you would leave me."

understand us

Christ replied, "My precious, precious child, I love you and I would never leave you. During your times of trial and suffering, when you see only one set of footprints, it was then that I carried you."

Author unknown

comfort us

HOLY, HOLY, HOLY

In the year that King Uzziah died, I saw God sitting on a throne, high and lofty; and the hem of God's robe filled the temple. Seraphs were in attendance above God. And one called to another and said: "Holy, holy, holy is the God of hosts; the whole earth is full of God's glory."

Isaiah 6:1–2a, 3

Manuscript illumination, *The Vision of Isaiah*, c. 1000, Staatsbibliothek, Bamberg, Germany. Used by permission.

What do you see in this picture?

What in it illustrates the words from Isaiah?

What is in the painting that is not mentioned in Isaiah?

**"Holy, holy, holy is the God of hosts;
the whole earth is full of God's glory."**

In mystery and grandeur
we see the face of God
in earthiness and the ordinary
we know the love of Christ.

In heights and depths
and life and death:
the spirit of God
is moving among us.

Let us praise God.

I will light a light
in the name of God
who lit the world
and breathed the breath of life into me.

I will light a light
in the name of the Son
who saved the world
and stretched out his hand to me.

I will light a light
in the name of the Spirit
who encompasses the world
and blesses my soul with yearning.

We will light three lights
for the trinity of love:
God above us,
God beside us,
God beneath us:
the beginning,
the end,
the everlasting one.

Michael Shaw and Paul Indwood, "Litany of the Spirit,"
in *In Spirit and in Truth* (London: St. Thomas More Centre,
1978), 7. Used by permission.

How do you imagine God?

....

....

....

....

Where do you picture this God living or being?

....

....

....

....

How do you respond to the God whose glory fills the whole earth?

....

....

....

....

On the Sabbath?

One sabbath Jesus was going through the grainfields; and as they made their way the disciples began to pluck heads of grain. The Pharisees said to Jesus, "Look, why are they doing what is not lawful on the sabbath?"

Mark 2:23–24

Ben Shahn, *Beatitude*, 1952, private collection. Used by permission of VAGA.

The Sabbath . . .

For Jews it is the seventh day, Saturday,

and for most Christians it is the first day, Sunday.

In either case, it is a day set aside from the other six

as the day which God . . . blessed and hallowed.

Frederick Buechner, *Wishful Thinking: A Seeker's ABC*, revised and expanded edition (San Francisco: HarperSan Francisco, 1973), 100. Copyright © 1973 by Frederick Buechner. Used by permission of HarperCollins Publishers, Inc.

Right side of the room:

I give you thanks, O God, with my whole heart; I sing your praise!

Left side of the room:

I give you thanks, O God. I bow down; I sing your praise!

All:

For you have searched me and known me. You know the conflicts of my life. You know my desire to follow your way of love and compassion.

Women:

Though I walk in the midst of trouble, you stretch out your hand of love and compassion to me.

Men:

Though I walk in the midst of trouble, your hand of love and compassion delivers me.

All:

You continue to search me and know me. You are acquainted with all my ways, and you lay your hand upon me.

Those with January–June birthdays:

You have answered my calls and increased my strength of soul.

Those with July–December birthdays:

You will fulfill your purpose for me; your steadfast love, O God, endures forever.

All:

We go forth into the world blessed with God's love and compassion. We go forth into the world ready to share that love and compassion in the strength of God's faithfulness.

Adapted from Psalms 138 and 139

The eternal

For what can be seen is temporary . . .

Christo and Jeanne-Claude, *Running Fence, Sonoma and Marin Counties, California*, 1972–1976.
Photo by Jeanne-Claude. © Christo. Used by permission.

Because we look not at what can be seen but at what cannot be seen; for what
can be seen is temporary, but what cannot be seen is eternal. For we know that if
the earthly tent we live in is destroyed, we have a building from God, a house not
made with hands, eternal in the heavens.

2 Corinthians 4:18–5:1 . . . but what cannot be seen
is eternal.

What the fox said to the Little Prince:

"And now here is my secret,

a very simple secret:

It is only with the heart

that one can see rightly;

what is essential is invisible

to the eye."

Antoine De Saint-Exupery, *The Little Prince*, trans. Katherine Woods
(New York: Harcourt, Brace and World, 1943), 87.

I have recovered it.

What? Eternity.

You promise to all who trust you

It is the sea

forgiveness of sins and fullness of grace,

Matched with the sun.

courage in the struggle for justice and peace,

Arthur Rimbaud, excerpt from "Eternity,"
trans. Francis Golffing, in *Prentice Hall Literature:
World Masterpieces* (New York: Prentice Hall, 1991),
910. Used by permission.

your presence in trial and rejoicing,

How would you draw or describe eternity?

and eternal life in your realm which has no end.

Excerpt from *United Church of Christ Statement of Faith in the Form of
a Doxology* (revised 1981). Used by permission.

Live by Faith

So we are always confident; for we walk by faith, not by sight.

2 Corinthians 5:6a, 7

Ben Shahn, *The Red Stairway*, 1944, St. Louis Art Museum, St. Louis, Mo. © 1996 Estate of Ben Shahn/ Licensed by VAGA, New York, N.Y. Used by permission of VAGA.

Imagine you are the person at the stairs. What are you thinking? feeling? What would it be like to climb those stairs?

Even the merest gesture **is holy** **if it is** filled **with** faith. Franz Kafka

97

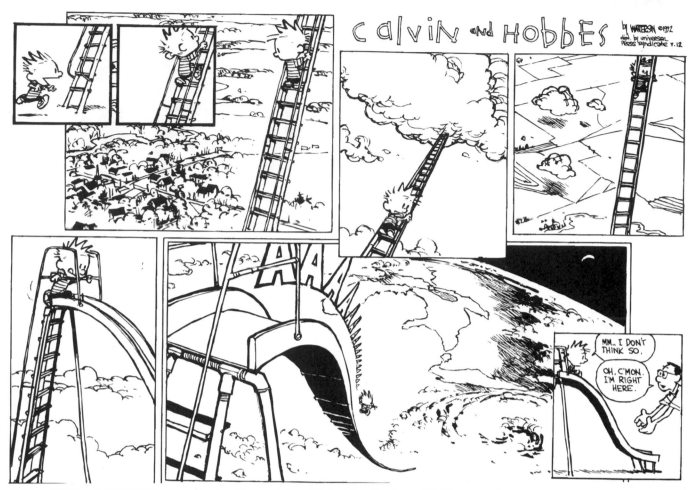

Confidence Quotient

Directions: Fill in each of the statements below to determine your "confidence quotient."

• I am confident that I will really enjoy a concert if _____ is performing.

• I am confident that a movie will be good if _____ is one of the actors.

• I am confident that the radio DJ _____ will always play great music.

• I am confident that news reported by _____ will be correct.

• I am confident that I can always talk to _____ when I have a problem

or feel uncertain about what I should do.

• I am confident that _____ will always be there for me.

• Who else (or what else) do you have confidence in? Why?

When you're at the top **of life's slide,
what gives you the confidence to** let go?

DAVID and GOLIATH

Manuscript illumination, *David and Goliath*, León Bible, Cod. I, 3, Pol 131, Léon Colequta de San Isodora. Ampliaciones y Reproducciones Mas (Arixu Mas). Used by permission of Arixu Mas.

But David said to the Philistine, "You come to me with sword and spear and javelin; but I come to you in the name of the God of hosts, the God of the armies of Israel, whom you have defied. This very day God will deliver you into my hand."

1 Samuel 17:45–46a

Man of Destiny
. . .
Young David, not an Israelite warrior at the time, figured the odds
and surprised everyone by calling the challenge.

The slow-moving Goliath
was no match
for the agile youth and his deadly sling.
David's shepherding days were over
and his career as a warrior was launched.

With natural battle instincts, and a flashing personality to match, the young warrior soon captured the imagination of everyone.

Mark Link, *These Stones Will Shout: A New Voice for the Old Testament* (Niles, Ill.: Argus Communications), 113–14. © 1983 Mark Link, S.J. Used by permission of Tabor Publishing, Allen, TX 75002.

HOW CAN GOD'S PRESENCE AND POWER HELP YOU TO MEET THE CHALLENGES IN YOUR LIFE?

A READING

Silly Sadako.
Silly Sadako, our Japanese/young/girl/sister,
  suffering from the injuries of a war in our
    nuclear age
  salvaging a war inflicted-scarring and marring
    disease.

Sadako was dying of war.
Yet, silly Sadako was still believing in peace.

You may know the story–
  Sadako believed in peace so much,
    that she knew, not thought, that
  not just perhaps/not maybe/nor if–
Sadako knew that by her folding one thousand
  cranes, peace would be at hand.

Silly Sadako.
  Folding paper into birds shouldn't/wouldn't/
    couldn't bring peace.
  But Sadako folded. Sensing the immediacy.
  She folded and folded, until, . . .
    somewhere around six or seven hundred
    of those birds,
      . . . she died of war, still believing in peace.

Silly Sadako.
  You didn't fold your one thousand cranes.
    Your plan failed . . .

Except that,
  people hear about Sadako's story
    and sometimes they are moved to
      fold a crane
  in papers; or in minds and hearts.
  A crane for Sadako.
  A crane for that same peace she believed in.
  And maybe a crane for that whimsy of hope
    we have for peace.
    That peace that's not rational/It will
      never happen/It's not possible.

Yet, there are the cranes that lure us to
  believe in a peace that passeth all
rational/human/techno/nuclear
  understanding that is more than possible.

Silly Sadako.
  You didn't bring about peace with your cranes.
  You simply kept it alive/keep it alive for
    people like most of us who are cynical
  enough to think it can't happen yet silly
    enough to think, well, just maybe . . .

Silly Sadako.
  You remind us that peace is possible.
  You remind us of the need for immediacy.
  You remind us of our need to work for/
    to expect/to know . . . peace.
  –a peace that surely is at hand,
  –simply needing to be believed/in reached for/
    embraced.

Silly Sadako.
  You keep peace soaring with your cranes
    made of pretty papers,
    made of committed minds and hearts.

Mariellen Sawada

GENEROUS ACTS

For if the eagerness is there, the gift is acceptable according to what one has—not according to what one does not have.

2 Corinthians 8:12

Stephen Shames/Matrix,
Mother Clara Hale at Age 87,
as reproduced in
The African Americans
(New York: Penguin Books,
1993). Used by permission of
Matrix International, Inc.

Clara McBride Hale's long career caring for sick children began in 1969 when a young woman appeared at her door with a drug-addicted baby. Before her death in 1992 at age 87, Mother Hale was a foster-care parent for more than four decades. She also founded Hale House, a safe, loving environment that has nurtured more than one thousand young victims of New York City's drug and AIDS epidemics.

What makes Mother Hale's gift of love to the child such a good gift?

What attitudes on the part of the giver make a gift good?

What attitudes on the part of the receiver make a gift good?

Then said a rich man, Speak to us of Giving.

And he answered:

You give but little when you give of your possessions.

It is when you give of yourself that you truly give.

For what are your possessions but things you keep and guard for fear you may need them tomorrow?

And tomorrow, what shall tomorrow bring to the overprudent dog burying bones in the trackless sand as he follows the pilgrims to the holy city?

And what is fear of need but need itself?

Is not dread of thirst when your well is full, the thirst that is unquenchable?

There are those who give little of the much which they have—and they give it for recognition and their hidden desire makes their gifts unwholesome.

And there are those who have little and give it all.

These are the believers in life and the bounty of life, and their coffer is never empty.

There are those who give with joy, and that joy is their reward.

And there are those who give with pain, and that pain is their baptism.

And there are those who give and know not pain in giving, nor do they seek joy, nor give with mindfulness of virtue;

They give as in yonder valley the myrtle breathes its fragrance into space.

Through the hands of such as these God speaks, and from behind their eyes [God] smiles upon the earth.

Sent by Jesus

Jesus called the twelve and began to send them out two by two, and gave them authority over the unclean spirits. Jesus ordered them to take nothing for their journey except a staff.

Mark 6:7–8a

Go

"Go Where I Send Thee."

Where do I need to be sent to make Christ's love known…

…in my world?

…in my community?

…in my school?

…in my church?

Haleluya! Pelo tsa rona
Halleluya! We Sing Your Praises

Words and music: South African

Refrain

Ha - le - lu - ya! Pe - lo tsa ro - na, di tha - bi - le ka o - fe -
Hal - le - lu - ya! We sing your prais - es, all our hearts with glad - ness are

la. Ha - le - lu - ya! Pe - lo tsa ro - na, di tha - bi - le ka - o - fe -
filled. Hal - le - lu - ya! We sing your prais - es, all our hearts with glad - ness are

Last time, end **Stanzas**

la. 1 Ke Mo - re - na Je - so, ya re du - me - let - seng,
filled. 1 Je - sus Christ said to us: I am wine, I am bread,
2 Christ now sends us all out, strong in faith, free of doubt;

To Refrain

ya re du - me - let - seng, ho tsa - mai - sa e - van - ge - di.
I am wine, I am bread, give to all who hun - ger and thirst.
strong in faith, free of doubt; tell to all the joy - ful Good News.

Children, Go Where I Send Thee

Children go where I send thee!

How shall I send thee?

Well I'm gonna send thee…ten by ten,

…ten for the ten commandments,

…nine for the nine all dressed so fine,

…eight for the eight that stood at the gate,

…seven for the seven that never got to heaven,

…six for the six that never got fixed,

…five for the Gospel preachers,

…four for the four that stood at the door,

…three for the Hebrew children,

…two for Paul and Silas,

…one for the little bitty baby,

…who was born, born, born in Bethlehem.

African American Traditional

Dance Before God

David and all the house of Israel were dancing before God with all their might, with songs and lyres and harps and tambourines and castanets and cymbals.

2 Samuel 6:5

The 1984 film *Footloose* tells the story of a teenage boy, Ren MacCormack, and his struggle to bring dance back to a sorrowing small town. In the following scene, Ren defends the senior class dream to have a prom. He shows courage as he challenges the town council's law against dance.

"You see, from the olden times, people danced for a number of reasons—they danced in prayer, or so their crops would be plentiful, or so the hunt would be good." Ren had started pacing back and forth in front of the council members' table. . . .

"People danced to stay physically fit, to show their community spirit. . . . And they danced to celebrate. And that—" He slapped one hand against the other. "—that's the dancing we're talking about. . . .

"Dancing is celebration! . . . It cleans out the body and the spirit, and energy that might be destructive suddenly becomes an expression of joy and happiness. For what? Well, for just about everything. For the fact that spring is here, okay? . . .

"Or maybe because we're graduating. . . . Aren't we told in Psalm 149 . . ." He snatched up the Bible. "'Praise ye the Lord. Sing unto the Lord a new song. . . . Let them praise his name in the dance.' . . .

How do you celebrate the presence of God?

Photo still from *Footloose*, Paramount Pictures, © 1984. Provided by Photofest, N.Y. Used by permission.

"And there was King David—King David—in the book of Samuel. And what did he *do*? 'And David danced before the Lord with all his might . . . leaping and dancing before the Lord.' *Leaping and dancing*, in front of God! . . .

"In Ecclesiastes, we are told, 'There is a time to every purpose under the heaven. . . . A time to weep, and a time to laugh; a time to mourn, and a time to dance.' "

"And there was a time for this law," said [a member of the town council].

Ren turned and, his eyes bright, met the challenge head on. "But not anymore! That time is gone. This is *our* time to dance. This is our way of participating in a rebirth. A new life. . . .

"That's the way it was in the beginning, the way it's always been and that's the way it should be, now and *forever* and *ever*."

Dancing in the Church

At times when faith and culture mix, the result can be a dramatically different way of praising God. Recently our Korean congregation in Kawasaki (between Yokohama and Tokyo) honored three women as *kwonsa*, a position of honor usually accorded older women in the church.

As a part of the celebratory party that followed worship, three teenage young women and their teacher gave a program of Korean drumming. Such performing on small drums, usually played while seated, is an important part of Korean culture. As the drumming continued, the teacher began to dance about the room in a Korean style that expressed the feelings of the joyful day.

Then, quite spontaneously, the oldest of the new *kwonsa* rose from her chair and joined in the dancing. Her movement encouraged others and one by one the other honored women joined her.

More and more women joined the dancing. Then some men began to dance. Now the rest of the congregation began to clap their hands with the rhythm of the drumming and dancing, until every single person was involved.

The spirit of celebration begun in worship had continued, as members of an oppressed minority shared from the depths of their spirituality and cultural pride. And in both worship and dancing God was praised.

Philip Park, "Dancing in the Church," in *Haiku Origami And More: Worship and Study Resources from Japan*, Judith May Newton and Mayumi Tabuchi (New York: Friendship Press, 1991), 88. Used by permission. (Philip Park is a Presbyterian Church (USA) missionary.)

Psalm 24:1–6

1 The earth is God's and all
   that is in it,
the world, and those who live in it;

2 for God has founded it on the seas,
and established it on the rivers.

3 Who shall ascend the hill of
   God?
And who shall stand in God's holy
   place?

4 Those who have clean hands and
   pure hearts,
who do not lift up their souls to
   what is false,
and do not swear deceitfully.

5 They will receive blessing from
   God,
and vindication from the God of
   their salvation.

6 Such is the company of those who
   seek God,
who seek the face of the God of
   Jacob.   Selah

Respond to these words of praise in writing or by drawing movements to an interpretive dance that celebrates the presence of God.

In One Body

Christ has abolished the law with its commandments and ordinances, in order to create in Christ one new humanity in place of the two, thus making peace, and in order to reconcile both groups to God in one body through the cross.

Ephesians 2:15–16a

The Wall Came Tumbling Down (New York: Arch Cape Press, 1990), 58. Used by permission of AP/Wide World Photos.

An East German border guard peers through a newly created hole in the once impregnable Berlin Wall.

Why are walls built?

Who builds them?

How can walls be taken down?

How has Jesus already removed walls that divide us?

Take the Barriers Down

The whole world is round as a ball

There's only one side to it.

We kill the world when we build a wall

We drive a barrier through it.

There is one earth, one life, one blood

We come from one another.

We only die when we try to live

Separate from each other.

(Refrain)

Oh Lord, oh Lord, O Lord have mercy.

Oh Lord, oh Lord, O Lord have mercy.

Let the war be over, take the barriers down.

Let the war be over, take the barriers down.

How can we live at war with life

Imprisoning our hearts?

Building a barrier, wielding a knife

We cut ourselves apart.

Men and women, rich and poor,

Life and all creation

Suffer from our fearful war

Cry for liberation.

Lyrics by Steve Garnaas-Holmes,
Take the Barriers Down,
The Montana Logging & Ballet Company.
Upstream Records, 1987, adapted.
Copyright © MLBC Publishing Co.
Used by permission.

5,000 Fed

One of Jesus' disciples, Andrew, Simon Peter's brother, said to him, "There is a boy here who has five barley loaves and two fish. But what are they among so many people?" Then Jesus took the loaves, and when he had given thanks, he distributed them to those who were seated; so also the fish, as much as they wanted.

John 6:8–9, 11

One Small Boy

The report
on the miracle
of the bread and the fish
is about what happened
to somebody who gave all he had.
It is, of course, a story about Jesus
multiplying all that bread and that fish.

Joseph G. Donders, excerpt in *The Jesus Community: Reflections on the Gospel for the B-Cycle* (Maryknoll, N.Y.: Orbis Books, 1981), 205. Used by permission of the author.

Alemayehu Bizuneh, *Scene X of the Misereor "Hunger Cloth" from Ethiopia*, Misereor Medienproduktion und Vertriebsgesellschaft mbH, Aachen, Germany. Used by permission.

How

How does Jesus' action show that he is God's Messiah?

God Is Rice

In the Bible there is a significant expression of God's love towards all people. It evokes the symbol of the daily sustenance of people. Jesus said: "I am the living bread which came down from heaven" (John 6:51). He taught us to pray: "Give us this day our daily bread" (Matt. 6:11). Furthermore, Jesus often illustrated the coming of the kingdom by the story of a banquet. To it are invited all people from the East and West. They are invited to share the common meal. And the night before he was betrayed, he took bread, and broke it, and distributed it among the disciples, saying: "This is my body given for you" (1 Cor. 11:24).

We tend to consider wheat, or bread, as the symbol of daily food everywhere. But to many Asian people bread is a foreign product. It comes from abroad. We Japanese had never seen this kind of food until the Portuguese missionaries and traders brought it to our country about the middle of the sixteenth century. . . . The most popular indigenous food has been, and still is, rice. We like rice. . . .

It is quite appropriate for us, therefore, to say "God is rice," rather than "God is bread." . . .

It certainly reminds us of the holy communion, which is the occasion to share our daily food together with all people as the symbol of eternal life. This has a social implication as well as a spiritual meaning. The Chinese character for peace (wa) literally means harmony. It derives from two words: one is rice and the other is mouth. It means that unless we share rice together with all people, we will not have peace. When every mouth in the whole inhabited world is filled with daily food, then we can have peace on earth.

Masao Takenaka, *God Is Rice: Asian Culture and Christian Faith* (Geneva: World Council of Churches, 1986), 16–19. Used by permission.

Where are you in this crowd?

Who do you say Jesus is?

What compassionate act can you do this week?

Jacopo Bassano, *Feeding of the Five Thousand*, Earl Spencer Collection, Althorp, Northampton, Great Britain (Bridgeman/Art Resource, N.Y.). Used by permission.

Growing IN CHRIST

But speaking the truth in love, we must grow up in every way into the one who is the head, into Christ.

Ephesians 4:15

Your unique and individual **mission** will most likely turn out to be a mission of **Love**, acted out in one or all of the three arenas: either in the Kingdom of the Mind, whose goal is to bring more Truth into the world; or in the Kingdom of the Heart, whose goal is to bring more beauty into the world; or in the Kingdom of the Will, whose goal is to bring more perfection into the world, through Service. . . .

Knowing that you came to Earth for a reason, and knowing what that Mission is, throws an entirely different light upon your life from now on.

Rembrandt Harmensz van Rijn, *The Apostle Paul in Prison*, Staatsgalerie, Stuttgart, Germany (Foto Marburg/Art Resource, N.Y.). Used by permission.

PAUL, EXERCISING HIS MINISTRY IN PRISON, WROTE LETTERS TO THE EARLY CHURCHES.

Richard Nelson Bolles, *What Color Is Your Parachute?* (Berkeley: Ten Speed Press, 1993), 370, 371. Used by permission of the author.

What gifts has God given you for ministry and service?

There are all different kinds of voices calling you to all different kinds of work, and the problem is to find out which is the voice of God rather than that of Society, say, or the Superego, or Self-Interest.

By and large a good rule for finding out is this: The kind of work God usually calls you to is the kind of work (a) that you need most to do and (b) the world most needs to have done. If you really get a kick out of your work, you've presumably met requirement (a), but if your work is writing cigarette ads, the chances are you've missed requirement (b). On the other hand, if your work is being a doctor in a leper colony, you have probably met (b), but if most of the time you're bored and depressed by it, the chances are you haven't only bypassed (a) but probably aren't helping your patients much either. . . . The place God calls you to is the place where your deep gladness and the world's deep hunger meet.

Frederick Buechner, *Wishful Thinking: A Seeker's ABC* (San Francisco: HarperSan Francisco, 1973; rev. and expanded 1993), 118–19. Copyright © 1973 by Frederick Buechner. Used by permission of HarperCollins Publishers, Inc.

What is society calling you to do?

What kind of work do you need to do?

What kind of work does the world need you to do?

Touch of an Angel

Then Elijah lay down under the broom tree and fell asleep. Suddenly an angel touched him and said to him, "Get up and eat." He looked, and there at his head was a cake baked on hot stones, and a jar of water.

1 Kings 19:5–6a

Do not neglect to show hospitality to strangers, for by doing that some have entertained angels without knowing it.

—Hebrews 13:2

For God will command God's angels concerning you to guard you in all your ways. On their hands they will bear you up, so that you will not dash your foot against a stone.

—Psalm 91:11–12

For a good angel will accompany him; his journey will be successful, and he will come back in good health.

—Tobit 5:22

And suddenly there was with the angel a multitude of the heavenly host, praising God and saying, "Glory to God in the highest heaven, and on earth peace among those whom God favors!"

—Luke 2:13–14

Then the devil left Jesus, and suddenly angels came and waited on him.

—Matthew 4:11

Dieric Bouts, *Elijah and the Angel,* Altar of the Last Supper, Collegiale, St. Pierre, Louvain, Belgium (Erich Lessing/ Art Resource, N.Y.). Used by permission.

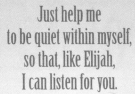

I am here, Lord.
I don't need to be alone at the top of a tree
to talk to you.

Just help me
to be quiet within myself,
so that, like Elijah,
I can listen for you.

Although you do not come
in a great noise,
I can hear you
and you can hear me.

Spirit of God, in me,
help me to pray
in the way best for me.

Joan M. Burns, in *Prayers, Praises, and Thanksgivings*,
comp. Sandol Stoddard (New York: Dial Books,
1992), 45. Used by permission.

Litany Adaptation of Psalm 34:1—8

1 Reader 1: I will bless God at all times; God's praise shall continually be in my mouth.

All: Let us go forth as angels!

2 Reader 2: My soul makes its boast in God; let the humble hear and be glad.

All: Let us go forth as angels!

3 Reader 3: O magnify God with me, and let us exalt God's name together.

All: Let us go forth as angels!

4 Reader 4: I sought God, who answered me, and delivered me from all my fears.

All: Let us go forth as angels!

5 Reader 5: Look to God, and be radiant; so your faces shall never be ashamed.

All: Let us go forth as angels!

6 Reader 6: This poor soul cried, and was heard by God, and was saved from every trouble.

All: Let us go forth as angels!

7 Reader 7: The angel of God encamps around those who fear God, and delivers them.

All: Let us go forth as angels!

8 Reader 8: O taste and see that God is good; happy are those who take refuge in God.

All: Let us go forth as angels!

SEEKING God's Purpose

Solomon prayed, "Give your servant therefore an understanding mind to govern your people, able to discern between good and evil; for who can govern this your great people?"

1 Kings 3:9

Jeffery Allan Salter, *Taurian Osborne Prays at the New Fellowship Missionary Baptist Church, Opa Laka, Florida.* Used by permission.

GOD SPEAKS TO US THROUGH . . .

God speaks to us through direct appearances.

God speaks to us through prayer.

God speaks to us through visions and dreams.

God speaks to us through the remembrance of God's prior actions.

God speaks to us through prophets.

God speaks to us through other people.

God speaks to us through the circumstances of our lives.

God speaks to us through the Word of God.

God speaks to us through Jesus and his teachings.

God speaks to us through our lives as they are lived in close relationship with God and one another.

Exodus 3:2–4
Acts 16:6–10
Acts 9:17–19a
Acts 8:29–38
Jeremiah 1:4–8
Matthew 26:36–46
Psalm 111:1–10
Jonah 2:4–12
John 6:51–59
Ephesians 5:15–20

As you look at the list, think about ways in which God has communicated with you. Which of the ways listed here have you experienced? You may want to circle them or write a comment about them in the space provided. You may also want to add other ways.

Think of one specific time God communicated with you. What did God want you to know or do?

How did you respond to God?

If you ignored this communication or didn't do much about it, how can you respond to God now?

Choose one or more of the scripture passages above to see examples of how God communicated with people in the days of the Bible. After you read the selected passage(s), decide where it might fit into the categories above. You may want to write the reference next to the sentence that best describes it.

Reveal yourself to us, O God, so that we might know your purposes.

the Vision Quest

The hard-packed ground was cool in the sweat lodge as Joe crawled inside. He had no time to think about it, however, for a forked branch holding a hot stone was poked into the hut after him. Twice more, hot stones were placed on the ground, and Joe pulled away from their heat. Then a pail of water was thrust into the hut and poured over the stones. Steam filled the small space as the water spat and cracked the stones. Sweat poured out of every pore of his body. He tasted salt as it ran down his face, and he blinked as it stung his eyes.

Hot! Joe was nearly fainting when the canvas cover of the lodge was jerked aside and he was pulled to his feet and dragged to the creek. "Yow!" he yelped as he forced himself to plunge into the cold stream. But then, a few moments later he felt like shouting and singing as he emerged from the water—he felt so joyfully alive, so clean!

"Now," the medicine man instructed, "you will climb the butte to pray and fast for four days or until your vision comes." Joe climbed the butte, dressed only in a breechcloth and moccasins and carrying offerings of tobacco. As the sun set, he lifted his arms toward its fading light and prayed. There, on the butte top—alone under the cold stars, the blazing sun, the rain, and the wind—Joe stood, naked, silent, and still. His body and mind were cleansed by the sweat bath, which also symbolically removed all the needs of human flesh, renewing him spiritually and physically. Sometimes he would sing, or offer the pipe, or pray. Eating and drinking nothing, he found time had no meaning—day and night became one, and then the Great Spirit sent him his vision.

Having fulfilled the traditional requirements for a Dakota/Lakota youth in order to achieve manhood, Joe returned from his quest with the memory of a vision that would guide him throughout the rest of his life. He received a new name and with it a new life as an adult among his people.

The Dwelling Place

Henri Matisse, Chapel of the Rosary of the Dominicans, Vence, France, 1948-1951.

Photo by Hélène Adant. Used by permission of Soeur Jacques Marie, Chapelle de Vence.

Then Solomon stood before the altar of God in the presence of all the assembly of Israel, and spread out his hands to heaven: "Hear the plea of your servant and of your people Israel when they pray toward this place; O hear in heaven your dwelling place; heed and forgive."

1 Kings 8:22, 30

where do you find the "dwelling place" of God today?

117

As you enter into these sacred spaces, what do you

see, or feel, or smell, or taste, or hear

that makes them sacred for you?

This is the sanctuary of First Church of Christ, Congregational, New Britain, Connecticut.

This *kiva*, the ceremonial worship space of the Pueblo people, is located in Kuana, Coronado State Monument, New Mexico.

Psalm 84

**How lovely is your dwelling place,
O God of Hosts!
My soul longs, indeed it faints
for the courts of God;
my heart and my flesh sing for joy
to the living God.**

Psalm 84:1-2

Large bells under a thatched roof ring out, calling worshipers to this sacred space by the sea in Mexico.

Doers of the Word

But be doers of the word, and not merely hearers who deceive themselves.

James 1:22

Jana Norman-Richardson. Used by permission.

Doing the Word

Not one of the youth from the First Congregational Church in Winter Park, Florida, or Plymouth Congregational Church in Miami, Florida, knew much about construction. And yet, there they were together at ICARE, the Interfaith Coalition for Andrew Relief Efforts, in Homestead. It had been three years since Hurricane Andrew had destroyed thousands of homes in this south Florida town, and several hundred homes remained in desperate need of repair. That's what the two youth groups were there to do. Even though they believed in what they were doing, because the Bible says so much about helping others in need, the youth weren't very confident about how much help they could actually be.

After several days of painting, roofing, insulating, and laying carpet under the close supervision of the ICARE staff, the youth from these two Florida churches knew a lot more about construction than they had ever dreamed of knowing. And they also knew that they had put their faith into action: they were doers of the Word.

Jana Norman-Richardson

How can your youth group be **doers of the Word?**

"Just like we helped rebuild people's houses, God helps people rebuild their lives."

Chris C., age 13

"Jesus taught us to help people because that's what he did. We preached the gospel through our helping."

Mariah B., age 13

"ICARE helped me get in touch with the idea of helping others as a part of faith. I felt like we weren't just helping people, but we were helping people because we're Christians— we helped in a Christian way."

Clay C., age 14

Things to do :

Reflect on what you have heard from God's Word this week. Then list things you will do this week among your family and friends that can connect to things you have heard from God's Word. For instance, you can speak a word of forgiveness or give a gift of love.

Let every word
be the fruit
of action and reflection.
Reflection alone
without action
or tending toward it
is mere theory,
adding its weight
when we are
overloaded
with it already.
Action alone
without reflection
is being busy
pointlessly.
Honor the Word eternal
and speak
to make
a new world possible.

Helder Camara, *The Desert Is Fertile* (Maryknoll, N.Y.: Orbis Books, 1974). Used by permission. (IF THIS IS POETRY, PERMISSION MUST BE SOUGHT.)